"This is a significant book at the time of widespread uncertainty and confusion in architectural theory, education and practice"
Juhani Pallasmaa, architect and author of The Eyes of the Skin

"In this timely and important study, David Scheer offers a lucid analysis of a dramatic, unprecedented, epistemological shift in architecture and its production"
Michael Sorkin, architecture critic, Distinguished Professor of Architecture and Director of the Graduate Program in Urban Design, City College of New York

"David Scheer offers a clear and unvarnished assessment of what architects have to lose and gain as we move from representative to simulated experiences, from controlling to collaborative practices, and from Euclidean to parametric/algorithmic form-making"
Thomas Fisher, author of Designing to Avoid Disaster, *professor of architecture and the Dean of the College of Design, University of Minnesota*

"David Scheer's important book on the role of drawing in the digital and virtual age reminds us that the actual relationship between the hand and the mind is neither casual nor expendable"
Renata Hejduk, Assistant Professor of Architectural History and Theory in the School of Architecture, Arizona State University

THE DEATH OF DRAWING

The Death of Drawing explores the causes and effects of the epochal shift from drawing to computation as the chief design and communication medium in architecture. Drawing both framed the thinking of architects and organized the design and construction process to place architects at its center. Its displacement by building information modeling (BIM) and computational design recasts both the terms in which architects think and their role in building production. Author David Ross Scheer explains that, whereas drawing allowed architects to represent ideas in form, BIM and computational design simulate experience, making building behavior or performance the primary object of design.

The author explores many ways in which this displacement is affecting architecture: the dominance of performance criteria in the evaluation of design decisions; the blurring of the separation of design and construction; the undermining of architects' authority over their projects by automated information sharing; the elimination of the human body as the common foundation of design and experience; the transformation of the meaning of geometry when it is performed by computers; the changing nature of design when it requires computation or is done by a digitally-enabled collaboration. Throughout the book, Scheer examines both the theoretical bases and the practical consequences of these changes.

The Death of Drawing is a clear-eyed account of the reasons for and consequences of the displacement of drawing by computational media in architecture. Its aim is to give architects the ability to assess the impact of digital media on their own work and to see both the challenges and opportunities of this historic moment in the history of their discipline.

The Death of Drawing is accompanied by a blog and forum at DeathOf Drawing.com. The site features the book's illustrations in color and offers interested readers the opportunity to initiate and participate in discussions related to the book.

David Ross Scheer received his Master of Architecture degree from Yale University in 1984. He brings a broad background in practice, teaching and research to his thinking about the effects of digital technologies on architecture. He has taught architectural design, history and theory at several schools of architecture around the U.S. and has lectured and written extensively on building information modeling (BIM). He has explored the uses of BIM and other digital technologies in his practice for nearly twenty years. As a longstanding member of the advisory group of the AIA Technology in Architectural Practice Knowledge Community (and its Chair in 2012), Mr. Scheer has gained a broad awareness of the evolving uses and effects of BIM and computation throughout the building industry.

THE DEATH OF DRAWING

DRAWING

Architecture in the Age of Simulation

David Ross Scheer

Routledge
Taylor & Francis Group

LONDON AND NEW YORK

First published 2014
by Routledge
711 Third Avenue, New York, NY 10017

and by Routledge
2 Park Square, Milton Park, Abingdon, Oxon OX14 4RN

Routledge is an imprint of the Taylor & Francis Group, an informa business

© 2014 Taylor & Francis

The right of David Ross Scheer to be identified as author of this work has been asserted by him in accordance with sections 77 and 78 of the Copyright, Designs and Patents Act 1988.

Front cover image, paperback edition: Wesley Taylor, sketch of the "Spirit Bell" (2008). Part of a competition entry for the Contrabands & Freedmen's Cemetery Memorial.

Library of Congress Cataloging in Publication Data
Scheer, David R.
   The death of drawing : architecture in the age of simulation / David Scheer.
      pages cm
   Includes index.
   1. Architectural design. 2. Architectural drawing—Psychological aspects.
   3. Building information modeling—Psychological aspects. I. Title.
   NA2750.S34 2014
   720.28'4—dc23   2013035065

ISBN: 978-0-415-83495-7 (hbk)
ISBN: 978-0-415-83496-4 (pbk)
ISBN: 978-1-315-81395-0 (ebk)

Acquisition Editor: Wendy Fuller
Editorial Assistant: Emma Gadsden
Production Editor: Jennifer Birtill
Typesetter: Keystroke, Station Road, Codsall, Wolverhampton
Typeset in Times

For my mother, Lynne Ross Scheer,
who loved champagne and ideas.

Frontispiece, Karl Friedrich Schinkel, "Die Erfindung der Zeichenkunst" ("The Origin of Draftsmanship," 1830). This painting depicts a story by Pliny the Elder about a girl named Diboutades who traces the shadow of her departing lover as a keepsake. This story has been taken up by many painters as an allegory for the origin of painting. In Schinkel's interpretation, however, it is used to describe the nature of architectural drafting. As Robin Evans points out in *The Projective Cast*, at least three features indicate this. First, the light is that of the sun which casts parallel rays, making the shadow an orthographic projection. Second, there are no buildings in Schinkel's painting, indicating that drawing must precede building. Finally, Diboutades is not making the drawing, but directing someone else, reflecting the distinction between the vision of the architect and its translation into drawing.

Source: Image courtesy of von der Heydt Museum, Wuppertal.

CONTENTS

ACKNOWLEDGMENTS

I owe a deep debt of gratitude to many people who helped me with this book. I'd first like to thank those people who gave generously of their time to read drafts of chapters or the entire book which was a painful chore indeed: Chuck Eastman, Ole Fischer, Daniel Friedman, Dan Hoffman, and Michael Sorkin. Their comments and insights were more valuable than they'll ever know. I owe special thanks to Shundana Yusaf who took me under her wing as if I were her graduate student, providing detailed comments and offering many insightful critiques and suggestions.

I especially want to thank several people who inspired me by contributing beautiful, eloquent drawings that show that the art is alive and well in current practice: Terry Dwan, Elizabeth Gamard, Hyun Joo Lee, Aarti Kathuria, Frank Lupo, Bryan Shiles, Wesley Taylor, and Sarah Willmer. Equal thanks are due to architects who allowed me to include their projects:

"Bilder Pavilion": Achim Menges/ICD/ITKE University of Stuttgart.
"Learning from Candela": Shajay Bhooshan, Alicia Nahmad, Joshua Zabel, Knut Brunier, and Mustafa El Sayed.
"Lotus 7.0": Studio Roosegaarde.
"Minimal Complexity": Vlad Tenu.

"Galapagos": John Locke.
"Reactive Grip": William Provancher/Haptic Lab.
"Solar Carve": Studio Gang Architects.
"Terriform": Ahmed Abouelkheir/35Degree Team.

I also want to thank my research assistant Ruth Mandel for her invaluable help finding and obtaining the rights to many of the images. In this connection, special thanks are due to Terry Dwan for her persistent efforts negotiating with several Italian sources and to Vicente del Rio for his help gaining access to Alvaro Siza.

For countless conversations and stimulations on the subject of technology and architecture, I want to thank my colleagues in the Technology in Architectural Practice Knowledge Community of the AIA: Luciana Burdi, Chuck Eastman, Pete Evans, Kristine Fallon, Steve Hagan, Calvin Kam, Mike Kenig, Karen Kensek, Kimon Onuma, Jeff Ouellette, Tony Rinella, Brian Skripac, and Andy Smith.

Finally, to Brenda Scheer, my wife, partner in practice and fellow inquiring spirit: my deepest appreciation for the conversations, provocations and never-flagging support.

INTRODUCTION

I

Like many architects, my enjoyment of drawing played a large part in my choice of career. I like the feel of a soft pencil on good sketch paper, like the texture of finely ground coffee between my fingers. I like watching and feeling my hand find a form on paper I hardly knew I had in my mind. I even like the laborious process of making presentation and working drawings, the slow, fastidious accretion of marks that leads to a supremely satisfying result. In architecture school, I studied the drawings of architects past and present, and came to feel that I understood them by the way they drew. I embraced the idea that my drawings should demonstrate the qualities I wanted my buildings to have. And I earned my living for several years by my skill as a draftsman, of which I was quite proud. Years later, when I started my own firm, I surrounded myself with people who drew well and resisted CAD as long as I could. When I finally decided I could hold out no longer, I shopped around and found something cool and (at the time) unique: a computer program that would allow us to create "three-dimensional" models and then produce drawings by "cutting" them. The term did not exist at the time, but I had discovered building information modeling, or BIM. BIM allowed my small firm to do more and larger projects than would have been possible with CAD, let alone hand-drafting. We made fewer mistakes because the drawings were automatically coordinated. And we had some kind of fun watching our projects develop in 3-D.

Fast forward 16 years: BIM is being widely adopted throughout the building industry. Our world is being turned upside down as BIM and other digital technologies transform the professional landscape. Younger architects and students immerse themselves in virtual worlds and few learn to draw as I did. Older architects struggle to understand how best to use these technologies and keep their firms competitive. Our profession is changing dramatically even as we go about our daily work. Things are changing so fast that few architects have time to reflect on what, exactly, is going on. Based on my experience using and teaching these technologies, and taking part in discussions about them with building professionals and technologists from all over the world, I believe that we are in the midst of a transformation that will ultimately reshape architecture to an extent not seen in over 500 years. This experience has also shown me that very few architects appreciate the magnitude of this sea change. These technologies are not "another pencil;" they are both evidence and agents of fundamental changes in the nature of architecture. These changes reflect the incorporation of architecture and the building industry as a whole into a pervasive social and cultural movement towards virtualization and predictive control through digital simulation. Architects need to understand why this is happening and its effects on how we think and work if we want to continue shape the design of the built environment. This, in a nutshell, is the purpose of this book.

II

The modern profession of architecture was invented during the Renaissance, due largely to Leon Battista Alberti and his epochal book *De Re Aedificatoria* (*On Building*). The revolutionary idea at the heart of this book was that the architect's role is to design, not to build. Architecture became a purely intellectual endeavor and the architect's proper domain of knowledge was what we would call theory: the reasons *why* buildings should be designed in certain ways. Furthermore, following Aristotle, Alberti deemed this knowledge of "why" to be superior to the builder's knowledge of "how," placing the architect above the builder as the true author of a building. Drawing became essential to architecture as the expression of architectural ideas, the architect's work product and the link between thought, design and construction.

Drawing in architecture has two essential aspects: as medium and as craft. As a medium, it provides the basis for both architectural ideation and signification. Representing three spatial dimensions by two requires the architect to establish an imaginative connection between a drawing and the building it represents. This ability takes years to develop. Drawing provides the structure for the architect's thought, as vague ideas begin to take shape on the page. It can do this in a practically infinite number of ways, and the architect can choose among various types of drawing and different media to develop a particular idea. It is in this imaginative space between idea and drawing that design truly takes place. This space allows the idea and its visible representation to exist separately. It makes of the drawing a cloudy reflection of the idea, while the idea begins to take visible form in the drawing, which it must in order to become building. The work of design is to refine an idea by seeing what visible forms it gives rise to and allowing these forms to shape the idea so that it can more fully inform the design. Louis Kahn expressed this process well in his notions of form and design.[1] Form was his term for the ideal order that structures the building. Design denoted the visible manifestation of the form, modified by practical demands. Kahn allowed that a form could be modified to accommodate these demands, but only up to a point. If the distortion of the form became so severe that it obscured the form, then it was necessary to find a new form (Figure I.1). Form and design meet in drawing where an abstract idea about space encounters the realities that begin to turn it into the plan of a building. Drawing has the capacity to represent both idea and plan and so allow interplay between them. It thus becomes an essential tool for architectural thought. Drawing influences architectural thinking in several important ways.

Drawing trains the architect to think in *representational* terms. The marks on the sheet stand for something else, and the qualities of the marks exert a reciprocal effect on what is represented. In this sense, learning to draw teaches the architect how buildings acquire meaning. In learning to draw, the architect learns how representation works and gains direct experience of the interplay between an idea and its visible expression. Buildings so conceived are representations of the architect's ideas. Building is of course a very different medium than drawing, but it also involves the representation of ideas by visible forms. As architects gain

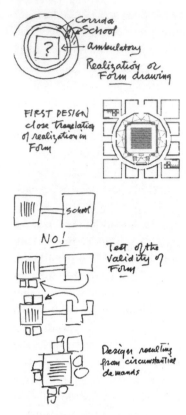

FIGURE I.1 Louis I. Kahn, plan diagrams and floor plan for the First Unitarian Church and School (1959). Kahn's initial, highly ideal, plan (top) evolves through a series of diagrams into a quasi-binuclear diagram that better accommodates the program. For Kahn, the form must accommodate the building's functional requirements without losing its integrity, or a new form must be found.

Source: Louis I. Kahn Collection, The University of Pennsylvania and the Pennsylvania Historical and Museum Commission.

experience in seeing ideas realized in buildings, they learn how buildings represent and this affects their drawing practice. Their drawings come to represent ideas that are capable of expression in building, creating an ever stronger tie between drawing and building.

Of all the aspects of a building, drawing emphasizes its form by its very nature. Architectural drawing was developed for the specific purpose of communicating a building's form to its builders.[2] Alberti believed that properly architectural knowledge concerned the means of arriving at the building's form. At the time, building construction involved a very limited palette of materials which the architect could rely on builders to understand. However, the architect not only did not need to tell the builders how to build the design, it was not his job—form was the primary object of his study and the result of his work. Over time, drawing has been adapted to changing conditions of building. New building materials and increasingly sophisticated technical systems obliged architects to include more information in their drawings, much of it in non-graphic form. The modern practice of detailing evolved as construction became more complex and builders needed more specific direction to carry out a piece of construction. These changes in construction technology have gradually enlarged the scope of the architect's responsibility. In spite of these developments, form has remained the architect's chief concern. Proof of this can be found in architectural magazines—the buildings featured there are nearly always remarkable for their form. This privileging of form in architecture has its historical basis in the Renaissance and the medium of drawing has been the key to its perpetuation.

The medium of drawing structures the modern building industry. As a medium of communication, drawing can communicate form very well once certain conventions are understood. On the other hand, only a small fraction of a building can be shown in a drawing set of reasonable size, so drawing places a premium on typical or repeated construction existing in many places in the building. This was not a significant limitation when building designs had a high degree of symmetry and construction methods were fairly constant from building to building. Now that asymmetry is the rule and each building can involve a unique set of construction methods, drawing effectively limits the variety of conditions a building can encompass. To mitigate this limitation, conventions have developed in the building industry governing what information is provided by designers and contractors respectively. These conventions allow designers to limit the amount of information contained in their drawings and rely on contractors to supply the rest. Thus, Alberti's separation of design from construction has been maintained in principle, although the purview of each has changed and expanded. The medium of drawing, originally adopted for its ability to describe form, must now be stretched to contain more types of information. However, the qualities of drawing as a medium still affect what and how much information the architect can provide to builders.

Whereas the medium of drawing has conspired in the separation of the intellectual from the physical aspects of building, the craft of drawing serves to unite them. Drawing is the skill which is the foundation of the craft of architecture.[3] Craftsmanship is essential to the work of the architect. To achieve the high levels of creativity and quality necessary for good architecture, the motivation to work can only come from an interior impulse, a personal satisfaction gained by doing good work. The work must be its own reward and the worker thoroughly engaged in the work.[4] This is the essence of craftsmanship. It is a shared sense of craftsmanship that underlies the profession of architecture.

The craft of drawing has traditionally been the hallmark of the architect. Involving as it does the mind, the eye and the hand, it builds understanding of its object on several levels. An idea that originates in the mind is expressed by the hand in such a way that the visible result is the product of both thought and action. The eye guides the hand, but the hand has, as it were, a mind of its own. The drawn form begins to acquire meaning through the body, as the building eventually must. As Juhani Pallasmaa writes, "[S]ketching and drawing are spatial and haptic exercises that fuse the external reality of space and matter and the internal reality of perception."[5] Sketching is especially important in this regard. Its inherent imprecision and immediacy allow thought to occur in real time as the hand seeks a shape that corresponds to an idea in the mind (Figure I.2). A unique kind of thought occurs while sketching. It may even be that the tactile experience of drawing gives the architect greater understanding of the architectural experience of what he is creating: "[t]ouch is the unconsciousness of vision, and this hidden tactile experience determines the sensuous qualities of the perceived object."[6]

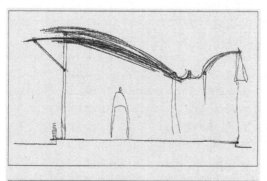

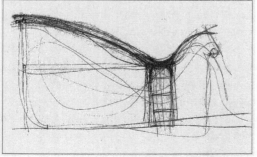

FIGURE I.2
Glenn Murcutt, sketches for the roof of the Magny House (1982–84). The architect's hand and eye search for a form.

Source: Glenn Murcutt. Courtesy of Architecture Foundation Australia.

FIGURE I.3 Steven Holl, watercolor sketch for the Knut Hamsun Center (1996). The choice of media for this sketch captures a quality of irregularity the architect wishes the building to have.

Source: © Steven Holl.

Furthermore, the hand is engaged with the physical media of pencil and paper and its action is conditioned by the qualities of those media. The architect's experience with the difficulties of getting pencil and paper to obey his wishes produces an understanding of how materials shape the ideas they are called upon to express. This encounter with drawing materials can be seen as a prelude to later encounters with building materials (Figure I.3). It teaches the architect to work with materials, to respect their qualities in finding a form rather than imposing one on them. "The work of the craftsman implies collaboration with his material. Instead of imposing a preconceived idea or shape, he needs to listen to his material."[7]

FIGURE I.4 Frank Lupo, elevation rendering for the Soling Competition (1984). Charcoal emphasizes the building's volumes and patterns of light and shadow. The superb control of this refractory medium is itself impressive.

Source: Image courtesy Frank Lupo.

As with any skill, learning to draw well requires years of repetitive practice. It inculcates values of patience, care, and attention to detail (Figure I.4). Making a beautiful drawing teaches principles of composition and cultivates an appreciation of well-made things. All of these values acquired in the process of mastering drawing carry over into the attitudes architects bring to designing buildings. A culture has grown up around these values that have defined architecture as a discipline and a profession.

Mastering this craft has been an important stage in becoming an architect and provided a significant part of the architect's professional identity. Skill in drawing has been the hallmark of the profession and contributed in no small degree to the authority and respect accorded it by clients and builders. In a well-made set of working drawings, builders can see the work of a master craftsman, analogous to the mastery they have achieved in their own crafts. The craft of drawing has thus provided a link between architects and builders and provided the critical nexus that unites the building industry.

III

This long tradition of drawing in architecture, with its influences on the thinking of architects and on the very nature of architecture, is in question for the first time since it took shape in the Renaissance. The divorce of design from construction, theorized by Alberti and realized in modern practice, is being overthrown by the replacement of drawing by *simulation*. Whereas drawing is based on a clear distinction between the two, simulation strives to eliminate any space between them. Whereas architectural drawings exist to represent construction, architectural simulations exist to anticipate building *performance*.

Unlike representation which rests on a separation between a sign and the reality to which it refers, simulation posits an identity between itself and reality. The nature of a simulation is that it mimics the behavior of some real system. To the extent that it does so, it can be taken as its equivalent in the operational sense. In the limit, simulation becomes indistinguishable from reality. That it rarely actually does so does not change this fundamental relationship. One approaches a simulation with the expectation that it will produce the experience of reality to some extent. Interpretation plays no part in understanding a simulation—the experience of it is taken at face value. Note that it is *experience* that the simulation reproduces—there is no depth behind the experience, no deeper meaning to be found. Thus, with simulation, reality is identified with outward behavior rather than with some kind of fundamental nature.

An architectural simulation behaves like a building—it gives the same results as a building when tested in specified ways. It is equivalent to the building in that its *performance* is the same. Building performance has many aspects: structural capacity, thermal comfort, energy consumption, cost, time to construct, functional efficiency, and conformity to building and other codes, among others. Once performance becomes the yardstick by which design is judged, every aspect of it can be viewed through this lens. Even its esthetic and experiential qualities can be viewed as a kind of performance that can be simulated and evaluated using the model (Figure I.5). Where an aspect of a building is difficult to quantify, the performative attitude tends either to encourage the adoption of quantifiable proxies or relegate it to secondary status.

Drawing and simulation entail vastly different attitudes on the part of the architect. In fact, the shift in attitude is more important for architecture than the actual uses of a given simulation. Once an architect decides to work in simulation, the values implicit in drawing no longer apply. As simulation tends towards an identity of model and building, it also blurs the distinction between design and construction that has been the basis

FIGURE I.5   Serta International Center. Photograph or simulation? Does it matter?

Source: Photo courtesy of Epstein Andrew L. Metter, FAIA.

of the definition of architecture since the Renaissance. The medium of simulation does not build an understanding of representation—quite the contrary. Simulation collapses the distance between representation and referent, establishing instead a functional near-equivalence. The representational aspect of building stands to be lost as architects lose the ability to think in representational terms. As a medium, simulation is immaterial. If a notion of craft exists in simulation, it can only mean ensuring the accuracy of predictions based on the model.

Creating a simulation requires the ability to digitally store and process large amounts of information of a wide variety of types. This information provides the data used by the simulation to compute performance. Therefore, the data must be *computable*, that is, the computer must be able to use it in calculations. Simulation thus requires casting as much building information as possible in the form of computable data—leveling the field so to speak and eliminating the disparate ways information is contained in a drawing. Having building information stored in this way has critical consequences for architecture and building:

- Placing all building information on an equal footing as computable data eliminates the privileged position accorded form by drawing. By privileging form, drawing made it the chief domain of the architect. Simulation does not favor one type of information over another. The architect emerges as a wielder of information rather than a creator of form.
- The availability of all building information in the form of computable data facilitates sharing it. In many ways drawing limited both the type and amount of information that could be distributed. By issuing drawings at specific stages of a project, architects could control what information was shared when and with whom. With all information in a readily transmissible form, there are great incentives to share it more freely, resulting in a leveling of the design team and a consequent redefinition of the architect's role within it.
- It was traditionally understood that drawings would lack a great deal of information needed to construct a building. Convention and practicality dictated what information was supplied by the designers and what supplied by the builders. In order to mimic the performance of a building in as many respects as possible, a simulation requires much of the information that was traditionally provided by builders.

Builders thus become indispensable members of the design team and the traditional separation of design and construction begins to disappear.

While simulation may be replacing representation throughout our culture as our mode of producing and consuming media,[8] architecture had to await the development of two digital technologies to permit the replacement of drawing by simulation: building information modeling (BIM) and computational design. It is only in the last ten years that these technologies (and the hardware needed to implement them) have reached a level of development that allowed them to seriously affect the building industry. In 2005, Thom Mayne warned architects at their national convention that they would use BIM or be out of business in five years. His timeline was too short, but the essence of his prediction was correct: these technologies will eventually replace traditional methods entirely.

The transformation of architecture that will be caused by these technologies is without modern precedent. The technological innovations of the 1980s and 1990s, computer-aided drafting (CAD) and computer-based visualization, while profound in their impact on practice, did not alter the relationship between design and construction, nor did they affect the professional identity of the architect. CAD left the representational nature of drawing intact. While many people have lamented the decline of the craft of manual drawing due to CAD, CAD drawings are still drawings in the sense that they depend upon the same representational conventions as their manually produced forebears. For much of its history, the impact of computer visualization on the design process was limited. Producing these visualizations was time-consuming and lay outside the workflow of the core design and documentation process. Making visualizations therefore cost the architect time and money, so that they were used most often to present finished ideas and rarely found their way into the design process. More recent technology has reduced the time required to make such models and allowed their incorporation into the design workflow, allowing visualizations to become more prominent in the design process. However, none of these technologies challenged drawing as the medium in which architects had to finally express themselves.

With BIM and computational design, architects have, for the first time since the codification of architectural drawing in the Renaissance, a truly new medium with a different epistemological basis. We can expect that, just as the medium of drawing affected architectural thinking, this new medium will have its own, very different effects. There are already many examples of buildings that would not have been possible to design or construct without these technologies (Figure I.6). Exciting new possibilities of building form abound, but there is some uneasiness about this new-found freedom. As architectural historian Mario Carpo puts it, "The economy of visual communication is dysfunctional because of an oversupply of variable images."[9] in other words, forms are meaningless when they are simply one choice in an infinite variety. What will become of the relationship of material to form? Louis Kahn's famous micro-parable about brick ("I asked brick what it wanted. Brick said: 'I like an arch.'") does not apply to new methods of machining, forming, and casting enabled by computational design. When designs are evaluated in simulations, will the buildings themselves become simulations of the simulations? If architecture loses the idea of representation, how will buildings acquire meaning?

Many architectural thinkers do not yet recognize the nature of this transformation. This is largely due to the fact that many of the most important aspects of this transformation are only apparent in practice while most thoughtful writing is done by academics. While a divergence

FIGURE I.6 London City Hall, Foster + Partners (2002).

Source: Photo by Arpingstone.

in the interests of academics and practitioners is hardly new, the situation created by BIM in particular needs to be understood from the perspective of practice.

IV

With regard to these technologies, the state of practice is presently highly diverse. This is due in large part to the current incomplete state of their development which can present many challenges for firms wishing to adopt them. The degree and sophistication of the use of these technologies in a particular practice depend on many factors. Clients' attitudes have the greatest influence. Some clients have chosen to promote the use of these technologies and may even require their use by the architects they engage. This is especially true of large owners such as the U.S. General Services Administration[10] that build and operate enormous building areas. Larger and more complex projects presently stand to benefit more from these technologies and have therefore been the site of their most advanced applications. In their current state these technologies tend to provide less benefit for smaller projects, particularly those that use a larger proportion of site-built (as opposed to prefabricated) systems. Architects' hands are being forced by the implementation of BIM by contractors who find advantages in using BIM for cost analysis, constructability reviews and construction scheduling. The adoption and implementation of BIM and computational design are thus highly uneven across the building industry and the architectural profession. It is clear, however, that the technologies, BIM in particular, are rapidly gaining acceptance.[11]

Despite the fact that this is a transitional moment in the adoption of BIM and computational design, it is important to ask what the ultimate outcome will be and what effects it will have on architecture. I believe that these tools will ultimately replace drawing as the medium of architecture and the construction industry. The reasons are explored in depth in Chapter 3, but briefly they are as follows.

First, there are powerful economic forces driving the adoption of these technologies. Major building owners have been plagued for years by costly problems with faulty construction documents and project management, and the logistics of managing vast amounts of real estate. BIM has demonstrated its ability to ameliorate some of these problems and holds great promise of providing better solutions in the future.

Second, technologies inherently tend to advance. As Brian Arthur points out in his excellent book, *The Nature of Technology*, technologies, once established, are systematically and incrementally improved as innovators seek advantages over their competitors.[12] The industry is witnessing this in BIM and computational design. Each year sees improvements in the capabilities of the software and the elimination of former obstacles to their use. The AIA's BIM Awards[13] bear eloquent witness to the rapid and remarkable expansion of the use of these tools by construction professionals to address an ever-expanding range of issues. These technologies may be imperfect today, but the economic forces behind them and the normal process of technological development ensure their eventual perfection. What they will be perfect *at* is another question and the major subject of the book.

Finally, BIM and computational design are part of a broad trend towards simulation as a mode of reception in western culture. Simulations attempt to reproduce as nearly as possible some experience of the real world, and in so doing blur the lines between medium and reality. Our experience of media is already largely based on simulation: we want media to reproduce reality to the point that the simulation is "as good as" reality and we adopt a mental posture which disposes us towards receiving media that way. Simulation has supplanted a mode of media reception in which a medium was understood to be something radically different from that which was represented by it. This shift has the most profound implications for architecture which will be explored extensively in the book.

The death of drawing referred to in the title has two meanings. In the first, drawing is the basis of the craft that has defined the architectural profession for centuries. The loss of this craft, or at least its passing from daily practice, will bring about profound changes in what it means to be an architect: what skills they possess, what role they play in the creation of buildings, and what defines their profession. In the second, drawing is a metonym for representation-based design. Representational design thinking is based on a system of signs and their referents, with the critical space for imagination and play that exists between them. Simulation-based design asserts an identity between the design and the building that forces the imagination to find other spaces for its work.

This book is an attempt to think through the foreseeable effects of BIM and computational design on architecture. I believe that this must be based on an understanding of three interrelated things: (1) the market forces driving their adoption and development; (2) the nature of the technologies and their likely capabilities in this time frame; and (3) the nature of contemporary architectural practice and its response to these technologies in particular. Like many earlier metamorphoses of architecture, this one has its roots in changing economic conditions that affect building. What is unique about it is that a response is being imposed on architecture from without. Whereas, for example, the Modern Movement was more or less free to shape its response to industrialization (and largely misinterpreted the historical moment), economic conditions today are forcing changes on architects. The technologies in question are powerful means of meeting new economic demands. The existence of the tools themselves enables and reinforces the economic trends. The tools thus become effectively obligatory for architects along with the changes in practice and thought they entail. The key question for architects is how the tools will develop: how architects will interact with them, their capabilities and, most importantly, their flexibility to allow architects to tailor the tools to their wishes rather than having to submit to the demands they impose.

This book will examine three domains in which the death of drawing will have profound consequences: (1) the profession of architecture; (2) the nature of architectural ideation; and (3) the role of architecture in our culture. The intent is to present an accurate description of the relevant technologies as they currently exist, to examine their effects on the building industry to date, and to speculate openly and rigorously on their possible consequences based on their likely development. Speculate is here the operative term. Technologies are developed by people, and while certain tendencies are apparent in the history of technology, there is always an element of choice. Architects can play a role in making the choices that will determine the conditions of their work, or they can watch passively as these choices are made by others. This book's goal is to stimulate debate about the future of the discipline of architecture and inform decisions about its direction.

Notes

1 Kahn (1991, p. 112 ff.).
2 Evans (1995).
3 As Richard Sennett (2008) writes, "[a]ll craftsmanship is founded on a skill developed to a high degree."
4 Again, Sennett: "The craftsman represents the special human condition of being *engaged*" (2008, p. 20).
5 Pallasmaa (2009, p. 89).
6 Pallasmaa (2009, p. 102).
7 Pallasmaa (2009, p. 55).
8 Baudrillard (1994).
9 Carpo (2011, p. 11).
10 See http://www.gsa.gov/portal/content/105075.
11 "The Business Value of BIM," McGraw-Hill Construction (2009).
12 Arthur (2009).
13 Available at: http://network.aia.org/technologyinarchitecturalpractice/home/buildinginformationmodelingawardsprogram/.

1

REPRESENTATION AND SIMULATION

One day several years ago, a discussion was taking place in an architecture seminar I was teaching. The topic was how drawings communicate. After some time talking about architectural drafting, I steered the conversation towards drawing in general and how the choices of media, technique, frame, and so on, contribute to producing meaning in a drawing. It wasn't going well—the students were a bit lost—so I asked them what the differences might be between a drawn portrait of a friend and a photograph of him or her. I expected that this question would get them thinking about the different kinds of choices one makes in photography and drawing and how and why they are different. But to my surprise, their answer was simply that the photograph would be more realistic than the drawing. I asked each one in turn to see if anyone had a different idea, but they were unanimous. I was amazed. How could advanced architecture students—presumably sophisticated about things visual—judge an image solely on its realism? Did they not realize that a drawing involves countless choices about such things as media, emphasis, exclusion and manner that are central to the artist's expression? Did they not experience such choices when they drew? I thought about it for a few days and then it hit me: they didn't think in terms of representation. The only purpose they understood for a drawing—or any other visual artifact—was to reproduce reality as accurately and completely as possible.

In other words, they thought in terms of simulation. It made sense: their social life consisted largely of electronically mediated relationships; their media world was almost entirely composed of simulations; in the studio, they designed using simulation software. Not only was the way I'd been trained and practiced architecture disappearing, but the very basis of all art as I understood it was missing. I suddenly felt very tired.

This was my epiphany about the extent to which simulation has displaced representation in architecture and society at large. It was also the beginning of an inquiry that culminated in this book. My central argument is that the relationship between design and reality is undergoing a shift from representation to simulation and that this shift has many profound implications for architecture. Both words have many common uses, but have very specific meanings in this book which this chapter will explain. It is very important for the reader to bear these specific meanings in mind in this and the following chapters.

Representation

Representation, as the term is used in this book, arises from the question of how human perception relates to reality. This question has occupied the minds of philosophers seemingly forever. Their answers have ranged widely, but there has been general agreement that we cannot know external reality directly because we have only the evidence of our senses, which are limited and unreliable. Therefore, reality must be *represented* in our minds in some fashion. Research in many fields (including philosophy, linguistics, art criticism and, more recently, neuroscience and artificial intelligence) has attempted to shed light on how our experience relates to external reality and how our ideas about the world arise from our experience of it. Representations condition our understanding of the world, setting its terms and limits.

A good place to start is the account given by Kant in his *Critique of Pure Reason* that has been enormously influential and is an important source of the idea of representation as used here. Kant accepted the notion that "true" external reality is unknowable by us. He believed that we create *representations* of reality based on our sensory experience, shaped by innate "intuitions," principally space and time, and mental "categories," such as causality and substance.[1] (Kant's ideas of intuitions and categories, as integral parts of the human mind, resonate today with research in neuroscience that gives evidence, for example, of brain structures that are hard-wired for language acquisition.[2]) Kant's theory implies that there is an inevitable gap between our thought and external reality. This doctrine establishes what is called the reality principle—that there is an external reality that exists independently of us and our perceptions (even though we cannot know it).

The question arises: if ultimate reality is unknowable, how can we become aware of the incompleteness of our representations? Kant's answer is that we have what might be called raw experience with which to compare our conscious thoughts. Experience is shaped by intuitions and categories but is (to use a modern term) preconscious. For experience to rise to consciousness, we must somehow represent it, but we are aware of it and of the distance between it and any particular representation. The common feeling that something "cannot be put into words" is a reflection of this. Thus, our knowledge of reality is always partial, in the sense of being both incomplete and biased. Our knowledge is biased in the sense that we often ignore the fact that it is incomplete and mistake our understanding for reality itself. The nature of a particular representation opens some aspects of reality to us and blinds us to others. The details of the construction of a representation are therefore of capital importance.

Kant was speaking about human knowledge in general. A specific representation can be understood as a set of *signs* that refer to reality, together with rules governing their use, as a language comprises both words (semantics) and syntax. A sign consists of two parts: a signifier, which is a physical thing, and a signified, which is a mental image.[3] In general there is an arbitrary (or "unmotivated") relationship between the signifier and the signified. Their association is a convention understood by a certain group of people. For example, speakers of English refer to a certain mammal that chews its cud by the signifier "cow." French speakers use the signifier "vache" to refer to the same animal, and so on for other languages. None of these signifiers has any connection to the animal outside the context of a particular language. However, there is a special category of signs (called natural or motivated) that have an innate relationship to the things they refer to, for example, the cross as it represents Christianity.

Many representational systems mix natural and ordinary signs. Architectural drawing is an example of this. Most of the graphical part of a drawing consists of natural signs, since the form of the drawing is a scaled-down version of aspects of the form of a building. Other parts of a drawing are arbitrary, such as the convention of representing a balcony above a floor level as a dashed line in plan. The words and numbers included in drawings are ordinary (conventional) signs as well.

Since we cannot know reality directly (only our representations of it), signifieds can only be mental images. The foregoing description of representation accounts for only part of the process of representation: how a representational system associates a mental image or idea with a physical object, such as a word (as a sound or a mark). The question remains as to how *signification* takes place, i.e. how we create meaning from this process. Mental images are themselves representations of reality; signifiers are thus two levels of representation removed from reality. Nevertheless, it is the signifiers we must use to describe reality, for others and largely for ourselves as well. How they are used (the grammar of language, the conventions of drawing) cannot but affect our mental images. Even the choice of one word rather than another to describe something matters a great deal to the image we form of it. If I refer to my dog as my pet, the image you form of it is very different than if I call it my service animal. In both cases you are thinking about a dog, but in very different terms. This also illustrates the fact that the meanings of both signifiers and signifieds are in large part the result of an implicit comparison among related images and signifiers (called *value* by Saussure). Choosing one signifier rather than another highlights particular aspects of the signified (more precisely, evokes a different but closely related signified), bringing it into a different network of related images and altering its meaning.[4]

This mental image conjured by a particular signifier is highly contingent on context and individual experience—not only will the mental images evoked by a signifier vary from person to person, but each individual's response is colored by his/her experience and the specifics of the situation: who is speaking, the context of the conversation, etc. Representation thus always involves a high degree of ambiguity. In any particular representation, some aspects of the object are emphasized and others suppressed or eliminated. In no case can the object be represented in its totality (otherwise we have the object itself which is impossible, as Kant showed). Ambiguity results from the disparities between the object itself, the mental image it evokes in the receiving individual and the limitations of the chosen representational system. Such ambiguity can make us aware of the disparities that inevitably exist between our mental images of an object or idea and aspects of our experience of it that elude our thought.

The inherent ambiguity of representation provides rich opportunities for creative expression. These occur when we become aware of some significant disparity between our experience and the available means of representing it. Exposing how a representation somehow omits, conceals or disfigures some aspect of our experience; asking a question about reality left unanswered by our representations of it; finding a new way of representing something that yields a new understanding of it—these are the kinds of strategies employed by creative minds (Figure 1.1). By

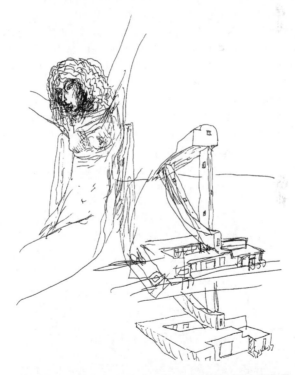

FIGURE 1.1 Alvaro Siza, sketch for Casa Baía (1974). Why did the architect juxtapose this female figure with an early sketch of the project? A formal relationship? Some association in his mind? Whatever the case, the combination affects how the sketch informs the project.

Source: Image ©Alvaro Siza.

exploring the ambiguity of representation we discover ways of representing aspects of our experience we have not been able to express before. That these representations are themselves often obscure and ambiguous is a token of the inability of any representation to fully describe our experience. Plumbing the depths of our experience and trying to come closer to expressing it in its fullness is what I take to be the production of meaning, a process that involves both the creator and receiver of such expression.

This kind of creative questioning of representation is largely the business of artists. When Edward Lear writes, "The Owl and the Pussy-Cat went to sea/ In a beautiful pea-green boat," a complex network of relationships among objects and actions comes to life through the words that represent them (Figure 1.2). Our normal understanding of an owl or a pussy-cat is shaken by the thought of finding them together in a relationship and an activity not usually associated with these animals. The image is both absurd and funny because of this incongruity. At one level, the situation Lear describes evokes our received ideas of the creatures by contradicting them. Since we associate their activities with people, the owl and pussy-cat are both anthropomorphized and made into metaphors of human beings. Yet they are not people, so the situation itself is thrown into question. Our ideas of owls, pussy-cats, boating and love (the two are revealed as lovers later in the poem) are transformed, however marginally, by creating novel relationships among their word counterparts.

FIGURE 1.2 *The Owl and the Pussy-Cat.*

Source: Illustration by Edward Lear.

As this example shows, thanks to the inherent ambiguities of representation, every utterance is an opportunity to question representation, to highlight and explore its ambiguities and to invoke other possible ways of representing the same or similar ideas. The ideas themselves change with their representations, so that there is a constant, gradual transformation of our thinking as we become aware of and question our representations. As we create ever-new representations, we in essence turn our experience over, examining it from an infinite number of perspectives. We can be sure that we will never exhaust the possibilities due to the unknowability of ultimate reality.

The incompleteness of representation provides other expressive opportunities. Since any representation is partial, choosing a particular one presents an object in a unique light. The aspects a given representation omits are not usually missed, they are just not part of that particular system. A line drawing thus is not "missing" shading or color, it presents an object *as* profile, as a charcoal sketch presents it as light and shadow (Figures 1.3, 1.4). Each representation describes a different aspect of the

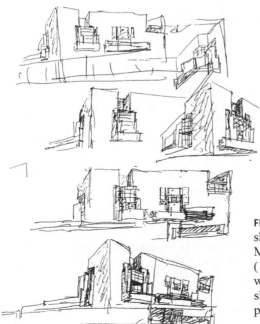

FIGURE 1.3   Alvaro Siza, sketches for the Manuel Magalhães Residence (1967–70). Line drawings with suggestions of shadows emphasize profile and mass.

Source: Image © Alvaro Siza.

FIGURE 1.4   Ludwig Mies van
der Rohe, Friedrichstrasse
Skyscraper Project, Berlin-Mitte,
Germany: exterior perspective
from north (1921). Mies's
charcoal drawing dramatizes his
project as bringing light to the
dark setting of the old city.

object, a different way of perceiving it. When an author chooses a particular representation, she is providing a clue as to how the audience
should understand the object. Comparing two or more different representations of the same object is a strategy for overcoming the shortcomings
of the individual representations. The totality presented by each is thrown
into question by the others; the viewer is left to synthesize all of them—
a compound or hybrid representation, as it were.

Architectural drawing relies largely on natural signs. Perspective
drawings are constructed using the rules of linear perspective. The result
is readily understood as a picture of a building. Plans, sections and
elevations, though never seen in an actual building, are imaginative
constructions of what one would see if it were possible to cut a building
with a plane and view the results from an infinite distance to eliminate
the apparent convergence of parallel lines. Another way to imagine
making such drawings is to mentally slice the building and impress the
elements in the cut plane on a piece of paper (Figure 1.5). However one
imagines the process, there are strict geometric relationships between the
drawing and the building that preserve the angles and relative sizes of
elements in two dimensions. Thus, perspectives and orthographic projections, while the products of imaginative processes, derive their form
directly from the form of the building, making them natural signs.

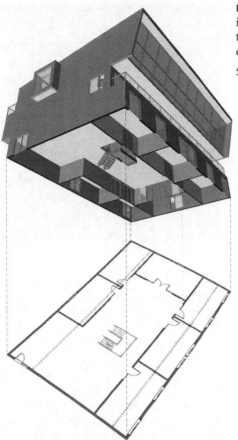

Natural signs are not without their distortions, however. In taking perspective drawings as pictures of buildings, we forget that linear perspective only approximates our vision. Furthermore, with different initial assumptions, equally rigorous perspective constructions can be made that appear distorted and do not lure us into seeing them as pictures. An extreme example of this can be found in anamorphosis (Figure 1.6). Thus, in spite of its apparent naturalness, perspective is actually a convention: we learn to overlook the disparities between linear perspective and vision in order to accept the former as an accurate depiction. Orthographic projections only appear natural to those whose constant use of this type of drawing (e.g. architects) have made the elaborate mental processes

FIGURE 1.6
An anamorphosis, a
distorted perspective
presented "correctly" in
this case by means of a
cylindrical mirror. Any
representation is a distortion
to some degree.

FIGURE 1.7 L.-B. Alberti,
Santa Maria Novella
(c. 1470). Renaissance
architecture assumed that
buildings presented
themselves frontally.

needed for their construction and interpretation so rapid as to seem to disappear. One fundamental way they distort what they represent is by naturalizing (reifying) the conventions that underlie them, such as the decomposition of an object onto two perpendicular planes. The idea of describing buildings through a combination of orthographic projections (not the projections themselves) arose during the Renaissance and responded to assumptions about the form and production of buildings that obtained at that time, such as bilateral symmetry, rectangular form and frontality (Figure 1.7).[5, 6] This system of describing buildings therefore makes these assumptions seem natural rather than the product of a specific time and place. In spite of the transformations projective drawing has undergone,[7] it would seem from typical building production today that the prejudices in favor of these assumptions have not yet disappeared.

Buildings themselves are (or can be) representations. Buildings not only give rise to experience in the here-and-now but also evoke associations, propose ideas and stand as the result of the work, intellectual and physical, of any number of people (Figures 1.8, 1.9). Like architectural drawing, buildings combine natural and ordinary signs. Also like drawing, buildings' seeming naturalness can mask conventions. Their apparently natural aspects largely derive from function and construction, both of which can appear as strictly logical responses to conditions they must accommodate. As pointed out by Karsten Harries, the naturalness of buildings' response to function tends to make us see them *as* function, obscuring the many other ways they may represent ideas and values (Figure 1.10).[8]

FIGURE 1.8 The University of Virginia by Thomas Jefferson (c. 1825) expresses an ideal of democratic education, gathering the professors' residences (which were also their classrooms) along an arcade surrounding a spacious green. The library at the head of the green evokes Republican values by its evocation of the Roman Pantheon.

Source: © Dalyn Montgomery.

FIGURE 1.9 At the opposite end of the political spectrum, Marcello Piacentini's Great Hall at the University of Rome (c. 1936) dominates the individual by its overwhelming scale and lack of detail. It is a clear expression of an ideology that subordinated individuals to the demands of the state.

Source: Photo by Phillip Capper.

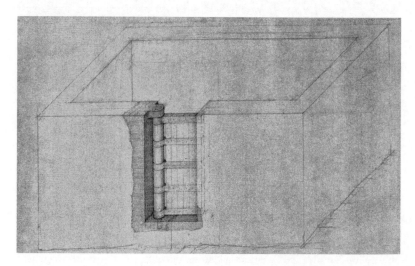

FIGURE 1.10 Walter Pichler, *Door* (1977). Re-presentation: a door that calls attention to its function by a reconsideration of how a door is made and the experience of opening it.

Source: Image courtesy Anna Tripamer.

Semiology's account of the workings of representation provides an idea of how the latter involves a high degree of ambiguity which can motivate questioning the relationship between a given representation and reality, often leading to new representations. This is a crucial aspect of representation as it enters the argument of this book.[9]

Simulation

In the ordinary sense, a simulation is an artificial environment that creates an artificial experience that is felt to be reality. Familiar examples include video games, theme parks, training simulators and historic recreations. Some are created by technology, some with building materials or other means (Figures 1.11, 1.12, 1.13). There are many entertaining movies and books that explore the dangers and paradoxes of a world where simulations are indistinguishable from the real world, where simulation and reality converge. However, there is no need for technologically produced simulations to create this situation. In fact, it already exists in our everyday experience as a pervasive mode of perception.

The connections between specific simulations and pervasive simulation can be seen by examining some qualities of the former. First, any simulation demands to be taken for reality. It *must* be taken as real or its

FIGURE 1.11 Electronically produced simulations may be what many readers think of as "simulations," but this is only one type of simulation.

Source: Gregorios Kythreotis/CC BY-SA 2.0.

FIGURE 1.12 Main Street at Disneyland, probably the best-known example of a physical simulation. To enjoy Disneyland you have to forget it is a simulation and live in the world it creates. Simulations are not always this obvious, however.

FIGURE 1.13 While not an overt simulation, the architectural backdrop of this shopping mall provides a vague image of a traditional Main Street that is intended to be experienced as simulation: an archetypal American commercial environment.

Source: © Brenda Scheer.

purpose is lost. If someone in a flight simulator thinks "I'm in a simulator," its training value is severely compromised. It only works as a training tool if the person in it believes (if only temporarily) that he is in a real situation. Conversely, the training will only work if, in an actual airplane, that person reacts as he did in the simulator. Simulation thus tends to erase the distinction between itself and reality, converting reality into simulation and vice versa, because they are both experienced as the participant's *world*. This is true even if the simulation is not very realistic.

Second, simulations are seductive and pleasurable. The degree of realism of a simulation is actually not very important compared to our willingness to immerse ourselves in the world it offers and accept it as our reality for as long as we choose to be engaged with it. This experience is almost universally found to be fun and enjoyable, a sign that there is something about a simulation that engages our minds on a very deep level. This indicates that human beings have a mode of perception suited to simulation, where appearances suffice and no ulterior reality is needed to make sense of experience. We do this even if the simulation is crude in its appearance. We can accept "worlds" without gravity, in which space and time are distorted, where actions have consequences utterly different than those we know. For that matter, we can accept as "real" experiences that stimulate only our sense of sight and overlook the lack of auditory, tactile, olfactory, and kinesthetic stimuli. As long as there is an internal consistency that we can intuit, we can inhabit any virtual world and enjoy the process of learning its rules.

Third, the means of producing an experience in a simulation can be utterly different from the processes that give rise to it in reality. The processes by which a simulation creates an experience do not matter as long as the effects on our senses are the same as those created by reality. A computer rendering, for example, uses algorithms that assign a number to each pixel in a display that corresponds (through another algorithm) to a color. These numbers are finally mapped (through the display driver— yet another set of algorithms) to the correct pixel on the display. This process for producing an image is not based on how images are created in nature, but is a totally different process that produces (approximately) the same result.

Finally, as a consequence, there is nothing "behind" a simulation other than whatever means were used to create it. In the world of physical phenomena, asking about how an experience arose, such as seeing a star twinkle in the night sky, may lead to discoveries about the cosmos, the atmosphere, optics, and other hitherto unknown phenomena. Asking this question in a simulation can lead nowhere that will deepen one's understanding of the experience or relate it to other previously unassociated experiences. The experience is a product of programming. The programmers of the simulation may create levels providing a sense of depth to the experience, but these will necessarily be finite and probably few.

Generalizing from these observations about the explicit simulations we are familiar with, we can see that there is a mode of perception that corresponds to simulation. Its essence is that, rather than representing reality, signs *become* reality, a condition called *hyperreality* by philosopher Jean Baudrillard. Representation preserves the reality principle— the idea that there is a self-existing world, separate from us, that always exceeds the ideas we construct of it. Representation relies on signs that refer to objects in the real world, while always leaving gaps and ambiguities in the relationship between sign and reality. Our awareness of these inevitable disparities contributes to the creation of meaning by stimulating thought about and exploration of parts of our experience that have thus far eluded representation. Simulation is based on an entirely different principle: rather than acknowledging and exploiting the difference between the sign and reality, *it replaces reality with its sign.* Simulation replaces the real with our perception of it.[10] Simulation equates a thing with its effects on our senses, its operation.[11] The operational aspect—the observable effects—of reality is the entire content of simulation. All a simulation does is to produce the same effects on (some of) our senses—the same experience—as a portion of reality. Anything we cannot—or do not need to—observe may be omitted from a simulation. From the perspective of representation, a simulation is a fraudulent representation that claims to completely reproduce a part of the world, fraudulent because all representations are partial. From the perspective of simulation, representation is eliminated, made over as simulation. In simulation, no external references exist —it is a WYSIWYG (what-you-see-is-what-you-get) world.[12]

Simulation is thus an orientation towards experience that can apply to any part of reality, whether it was created intentionally as a simulation or not. It has the potential to contaminate all of reality with its refusal of depth and reference. Simulation is viral: it can convert whatever it touches to simulation, like ice-nine in Kurt Vonnegut's novel *Cat's Cradle*.[13]

Once the identity of operation and reality is established, there is no stopping point. Representation and simulation are incompatible modes of experience. Either an object is a sign that points, however incompletely, to some external reality, or it is exactly what it appears to be with nothing behind it, so to speak. Simulation is anti-genetic: it deprives objects of origins or development. If indeed the modern meaning of explanation is to give an account of origin,[14] simulation denies such an account by limiting reality to appearance without regard for the mechanism of its generation (as in the example above).

As might be expected, the more we experience our environment as simulation, the more our cultural production reflects its lack of reference and depth. Designers, composers, and other creators of our cultural environment begin to focus on the immediate experience of their creations— the evocation of atmosphere and vague emotional associations—rather than on meaning. Techno, house, electronica and other contemporary musical styles directly engage the body through rhythm, relying on heavy, unvarying beats that annihilate time and thereby thought.[15] Movies rely increasingly on special effects and computer-generated imagery (CGI), placing these explicit simulations on par with real actors and locations, undermining the reality of the latter, subsuming the whole production into the regime of simulation. Architectural design manifests similar tendencies, from the frankly scenographic (Figure 1.14) to the diluted, sterilized historicism that characterizes so much public architecture (Figure 1.13).

FIGURE 1.14
This mixed use project attempts a scenographic recreation of historical architecture.

Source: ©
Brenda Scheer.

There is yet a third sense of simulation, as it is used in scientific research. In scientific simulation, a computer program is written that incorporates an hypothesis about a natural process, such as an idea about why the universe is expanding at the observed rate. The results of the simulation are compared with observational data. If the results of the simulation agree with the data, this is an indication that the underlying hypothesis may be correct—a *validation* of the model. The model can then be used to make inferences about other, related phenomena, producing new knowledge (Figure 1.15). There are several things to note here. Validation provides a connection between this kind of simulation and reality, ensuring that the former matches some aspect of the latter. However, while the simulation may give the correct result for one observation, there is no assurance that it will work for others. Additional validation is always required to ensure the greatest possible agreement

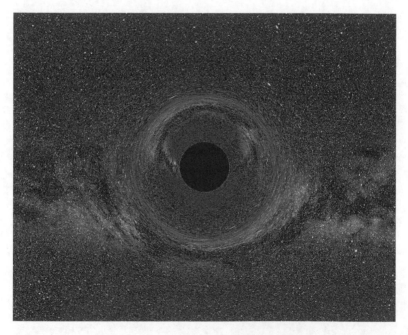

FIGURE 1.15 A simulated Black Hole of ten solar masses as seen from a distance of 600km with the Milky Way in the background.

Source: Kraus physics education group, University of Hildesheim.

between a simulation and reality. This process restores the reality principle to simulation – it is constantly reinforced that the simulation is subordinate to reality and is at best a partial view of it – it becomes representation again. Thus, simulation is as much an orientation towards experience as it is a process. The same simulation can be taken at face value by some and regarded as representation by others. Yet simulations are seductive by their nature. Although they know of the need for validation, scientists are often seduced by their simulations and fall into the mistake of reifying them, forgetting that they are only hypotheses and not actual reality.[16] If scientists, who are exceptionally aware of their thought processes, are susceptible to this, the rest of us are bound to be more so. The seductive power of simulation should not be underestimated.

Why has simulation become so pervasive? First of all, it is useful: as a research tool, as a design tool, as a means of communication. Used properly, it can predict the behavior of a physical system, the performance of a building, the experience of an environment. Second, it is pleasurable. The seductions of simulation are almost irresistible, even to people trained to understand its limitations. Perhaps, as with Burke's sublime, the pleasure of simulation is that we have exciting sensory experience with the potentially dangerous reality at a safe remove—in this case, eliminated altogether.[17] It appeals to our creative nature, allowing us to bring whole new worlds into being. Finally, it offers the possibility of a perfect world, one that works according to principles that we understand completely, having made it ourselves. In the words of Baudrillard: "[W]e are dumbfounded by the perfection of the programming and the technical manipulation [of simulation], by the immanent wonder of the programmed unfolding of events . . . The vertigo of a world without flaws."[18]

Simulation and Technology

Simulation technology was once as simple as stucco and paint, as with trompe-l'œil painting (Figure 1.16).[19] As technology advanced, so did the scope and realism of simulation. Media technologies, especially television, provided our first experiences of comprehensive simulation, giving us worlds in which we could live outside of quotidian reality. Further technological developments (computers, the internet, mobile computing, massively multiplayer online role-playing games such as *EVE Online*) allowed simulation to take over ever greater portions of our

FIGURE 1.16
C. D. and E. Q.
Asam, Church of
St. Johann Nepomuk,
Munich (c. 1746).
Detail of ceiling
fresco.

Source: © Author.

lives. However, technology is not only devices and techniques; it is more broadly a relationship between humanity and the natural world. Technology can be defined as "a means to fulfill a human purpose."[20] As a system, it is concerned with ends and not with means. Its purpose is to find a way to perform a particular task, with no regard for the means employed or its possible consequences.[21] Technology is represented as value-neutral and amoral in spite of the fact that its products often have profound ethical consequences. Any means of achieving the desired result is acceptable and the only criterion for preferring one means over another (as long as both meet the stated purpose) is efficiency.[22] This does not mean that technology only addresses quantities. For many consumer-oriented technological objects (cars and smartphones, for instance), an indefinable appeal to the consumer has great importance in their overall design. Technology subsumes such subjective criteria by finding a proxy for them that can be analyzed in terms of efficiency, in this case, profitability. In every case, the fixation on results (rather than means) and the criterion of efficiency dominate the process. Fundamentally, technology involves achieving dominance over nature. It permits human beings to reduce our vulnerability to the ravages of nature, to overcome the limitations of body, space, and time that nature imposes on us. Thus, the ultimate end of technology is to create a world over which we have perfect control.

Simulation produces results similar to those of technology. Whereas technology exists to dominate nature (which exists outside of ourselves), simulation supplants nature with worlds we can design to meet our every need and indulge our every whim, achieving the goal of perfect control over our environment. Like technology, simulation requires that we be satisfied with results without concerning ourselves with the means used to achieve them. Simulation thus shares and reinforces the values of technology. Like technology, simulation engenders and reifies the values of *performativity*. In this regime the chief criterion for value is *performance*, that is, effectiveness in achieving a specified result. Performativity confines the evaluation of objects, processes and acts to objectively determined criteria. Where performativity is the dominant value, there are no questions of truth or meaning, only of effectiveness. Metaphysics, ethics and ontology are excluded; the only question is, "How well does it work?"

Simulation and performativity are connected through the operationalism inherent in both. Performance is a close synonym for operation. Like operation, performance is only concerned with observable behavior. "Operation" is a neutral term for observable behavior. The term "performance" implies a critical stance. By regarding operation as performance, we set standards for it. As with operation, performance makes no reference to the methods used to achieve a result. Its performance is all we need to evaluate a method; it is exactly as good or bad as the performance it achieves; it has no intrinsic value. In this regime, value is assessed based on observable, therefore objective (i.e. intersubjective) criteria. In the context of performativity, operationalism, like simulation, also means ignoring everything that is not directly perceptible. Simulation thus limits experience to the domain to which performativity addresses itself. The beauty, if one can call it that, of simulation is that it makes performativity natural since it excludes by its nature all aspects of experience to which performative criteria cannot be applied.

Clearly, objective standards cannot be set for all aspects of experience. Performativity, however, only recognizes such standards. Experience that does not fit its framework must be represented by an objective proxy or left out of account. An example of this is the use of visual preference surveys as proxies for esthetic value (Figure 1.17). This avoids the vexing problem of dealing with the slippery notion of esthetic value *per se* by

A

B

FIGURE 1.17 An example of one of the pairs of images that make up a visual preference survey. Participants are asked which of the two images they prefer. Architects tabulate and use the results to guide and justify their design. This is an example of a quasi-quantitative method being used as a proxy for a fundamentally unquantifiable aspect of architecture.

Source: Marcus Hansson (Top); Matt Lemmon (Bottom).

replacing it with a poll of personal reactions whose results can be handled with familiar statistical techniques. This substitution equates the complex notion of esthetic value with the operational one of visual pleasure.[23] The need to objectively evaluate performance reflexively conditions the choice of the ends that can be pursued: only those whose achievement can be objectively evaluated can be adopted.

Performativity is a defining feature of our culture. As pointed out by philosopher Jean-François Lyotard, performativity plays a fundamental role in contemporary Western societies by justifying ("legitimating" in Lyotard's term) many of our most important institutions.[24] The performative attitude allows our judicial, educational, and scientific institutions to perform their practical roles effectively, avoiding endless debates about "esoteric" philosophical questions. We replace the abstract notion of justice, for example, with the pragmatic one of legality, which is a concrete product of judicial operations. We likewise privilege scientific knowledge above other forms since it is performative by nature. In science, explanation is equated with prediction. Scientific ideas are valued for their ability to predict observed behavior and for the generality of their applicability. The best scientific ideas are those that correctly predict the behavior of the largest number of natural phenomena in the simplest way. For society, performativity is itself performative: by avoiding ambiguous questions of principle, it allows society to function on a pragmatic level.

Simulation and Knowledge

The radically different relationships entailed by representation and simulation to the universe that exists outside ourselves profoundly affect how we think and what constitutes knowledge under these two modes of experience. In particular, the displacement of representation by simulation radically alters architectural ideation: what constitutes an architectural idea, how design problems are defined, how responses to them are sought and even the identity of the creator of a design.

Representation emanates from the fact that ultimate reality is unknowable by us and that representations are the only means we have of gaining conscious knowledge about the world. Comparing a given representation with our actual experience confirms the inadequacy of any representation to fully account for our experience and impels us to analyze our representations, identify their shortcomings and seek new representations to overcome some of these shortcomings. In this way, representation entails an endless revision of our knowledge of the world based on our experience of it.

Specific representations can also directly produce new knowledge. Representations include semantic and formal components. The former can be thought of as the "words"—the individual signifiers, whereas the latter correspond to the "grammar"—the rules that govern the use of the semantic elements. Manipulating the formal rules embodied in a representation can produce new knowledge about phenomena. Perhaps the clearest example of this is the use of mathematics in science. It is a remarkable fact that manipulating mathematical expressions can yield new information about the physical universe. Simply by following the formal rules of mathematics, explanations can be given and predictions made about the behavior of observed phenomena. Another example can be found in language. Unlike vocabulary, grammar (the formal rules of language) shows clear patterns, regardless of the language being studied. Psychologists and neurobiologists attribute this to fundamental structures of the human mind which can in turn be studied by studying language use.[25]

Although formal manipulations of representations can produce knowledge, the connections between them and natural phenomena must be established and constantly validated, especially when they are applied to new domains. Science has traditionally relied on observation and experimentation to validate mathematical predictions and, when irresolvable conflicts arise, these overrule the formal mathematical results. Mathematics is, after all, a representation and we know that no representation is perfect.

Whereas representations are always acknowledged as partial, simulations are total in that they become the observer's world for the duration of his/her immersion in it (it is no accident that we use words like "inside" and "immersion" to describe the experience of a simulation). Any aspect of the external world not included in a simulation is not, as with representation, held to be an omission or a fault; it simply does not exist within the simulation. Since simulation makes no reference to anything outside of itself, there is no way to discover its incompleteness. Simulation is experienced as the world and asserts the identity of experience and reality. It therefore cannot pose questions about a reality that may lie beyond.

Another way to view the essence of simulation is that it inverts the relationship between experience and model. Whereas representational models are generalizations of prior experience, a simulation is a model that precedes and determines experience. In the former case, new experience that contradicts a model forces changes in the model. In the latter, the model determines in advance what experience can be had. It is impossible to have an experience in a simulation that has not in some way been programmed into it.[26] Although the range of experience it allows may be very large and context-dependent, it is ultimately limited and preordained. We can therefore say that, on some level, simulation determines experience in advance. In its limiting effect, simulation can be compared to ideology. For someone in thrall to an ideology, anything that happens automatically appears to conform to the dictates of his ideology. For a Marxist, every political or social event is the inevitable result of the class struggle. For a religious fundamentalist, everything that happens is the will of God. The experience for an ideologue is predetermined by his ideology: whatever happens is an instance of its fulfillment. Similarly, the experience of simulation is predetermined, so that it always appears natural and gives no grounds for question.

Understanding produced by simulation is strictly operational. An operational understanding is one that is limited to observable effects. For example, most of us drive cars without knowing much about how they work; we are satisfied knowing how to make them do what we want them to do—the rest is irrelevant. It is the same, or more so, with computers. Our knowledge of these and many other things in our world is operational. Simulation as a mode of perception permits only operational understanding and cannot provide any knowledge about means or causes.[27] Simulations can be deceptive in this respect. Specific simulations can, and often do, have a kind of artificial depth that gives the impression of producing new knowledge. For example, motion in a simulation may be governed by the laws of mechanics, encoded in algorithms, allowing a user to "discover" these laws through the simulation. Such a simulation could be used to teach mechanics. However, the user has no way to know if the physics in the simulation works in the external world as long as she remains in the simulation. Without a connection to the external world, all the user can be sure of is that the "laws" she discovers work in the simulation, and the only use she can make of them is to manipulate the simulation. This is the very definition of operational knowledge. This may be repeated on several levels. For example, a car in a simulation might only be driven on a simple level, whereas a deeper level would provide an understanding of how the engine works, and an even deeper level would allow an understanding of the chemistry of the combustion reaction. However many levels are created, an end is eventually reached and the user is in the same position of having to accept the simulation as given.

For architects, this raises a pragmatic problem of having to trust the creators of their design simulations. Architects lack the time and skills to independently verify and validate their tools. They must rely on software vendors to do this, who often have trouble doing it themselves, since their products are the result of a long process of modifications, patches and other ad hoc measures rather than a focused process of design and development. Furthermore, there is a level of complexity, sometimes referred to as the "complexity barrier," which makes it virtually impossible for anyone, no matter how skilled, to verify a simulation.[28]

This pragmatic problem leads to a deeper one with implications for how architects think: having only operational understanding of their tools disposes them to accept operational understanding in other aspects of their work. This dovetails with simulation in general. The pragmatic conditions of their work and the general effects of simulation both lead to operationalism which transforms how they understand everything they do. The very notion of depth, of an ulterior reality behind experience, of representation in short, may disappear from their thinking. If that happens, the buildings they design will lack these things as well. The traditional grounds of architectural meaning will be lost.

Of course, to create meaning, there must be a competent audience, that is, people capable of discerning meaning in the expression of others. The permeation of our society by simulation raises the very real possibility that the bulk of the public already experiences its environment in the mode of simulation, regardless of that of their creators. This accounts for at least part of the distinction between so-called "high" and popular culture.[29] Creative people, including architects, who continue to think in representational terms are, to some extent, speaking into the void. Architects feel this perhaps most acutely because buildings do have performative aspects by which they can be evaluated. No one thinks to judge a painting by how well the paint adheres to the canvas, but buildings are often judged by comparable technical criteria. Architects thus often find themselves giving performative justifications for design decisions taken on quite other grounds.

On the level of the individual, representation and simulation are incompatible modes of experience. For the former, the world is composed of signs that refer to another order of reality. Ambiguity is not only inherent in representation, it provides a motivation to question representations and is therefore a vital means of producing knowledge. For simulation, signs are simply themselves, which is to say they are no longer signs. Any attempt to discover the causes of an experience in simulation remains within it. There is no middle ground between them: things either represent something else or they are simply themselves. For the time being, both modes exist side by side and a fundamental confusion reigns where they encounter each other. Architecture has resisted being overtaken by simulation longer than other forms of expression, largely thanks to the representational nature of drawing. Computational tools now provide an alternative to drawing, bringing simulation with them and finally aligning architecture with the culture at large.

Is representation good and simulation bad? The question makes no sense. These categories apply to historical phenomena. Representation and simulation are products of social and cultural developments in Western civilization which in themselves are neither good nor bad; they simply are. Neither are they fixed and unitary. Over time there have been many transformations within both modes and this will undoubtedly continue. As Daniel Mendelsohn writes, "What others might see as declines and falls look, when seen from the bird's-eye vantage point of history, more like shifts, adaptations, reorganizations."[30] What *can* be said of simulation is that it is a radical break with the past that creates, among other things, entirely new conditions for cultural production and reception.

Notes

1 Kant (1929, A 369).
2 Cf. Pinker (1994).
3 The following description is drawn from the foundational text of semiology, Ferdinand de Saussure's *Course in General Linguistics* (1983) (originally published in 1911).
4 This is what my students apparently didn't understand—that the meaning of

a drawing is expressed in the choices made by the artist to represent the subject in a particular way.

5 Evans (1995, p. 113).

6 Evans (1995, p. 119).

7 See, for example, Evans (1995, p. 324).

8 Harries (1997, p. 118).

9 It should be noted that, as a theory of language, semiology has subsequently been challenged and elaborated, with much work expanding upon the Saussurian notion of value—the determination of the meaning of a sign only in relation to other signs. This has led to a shift from the sign to the *text* as the relevant object of analysis, prominent in the work of such philosophers as Jacques Derrida.

10 As Baudrillard writes, "Whereas representation attempts to absorb simulation as false representation, simulation envelops the whole edifice of representation itself as a simulacrum" (1994, p. 2).

11 Baudrillard writes, "[The real] is no longer anything but operational" (1994).

12 Baudrillard (1994, p. 6).

13 In Vonnegut's novel, ice-nine is a fictitious form of water that instantly converts any other form of water into ice-nine on contact.

14 Foucault (1973, p. 227 ff.).

15 Inducing such a state of mind has always been one purpose of music, especially in ecstatic religious ritual. Compared with other forms of popular music, however, these styles are remarkable for their continuity with this tradition. Their popularity today is of a piece with simulation in the general culture.

16 Turkle (2009, p. 44).

17 Cf. Burke, *A Philosophical Inquiry into the Origins of Our Ideas of the Sublime and the Beautiful* (1756).

18 Baudrillard (1994, p. 34).

19 "[T]rompe-l'œil is representation's excess or its lack, its remainder" (Marin, 2001, p. 315).

20 Arthur (2009, p. 28).

21 Ellul (1964, p. 133 ff.).

22 This description is somewhat of an oversimplification: many technologies have to satisfy multiple criteria, making it difficult to decide which solution is best since optimizing all of them is impossible.

23 The visual preference survey (VPS) is often used in planning and urban design to provide guidance in developing design standards or actual designs. While its ostensible purpose is simply to determine what people like, the very decision to base design on this criterion already denies design any other purpose than providing a pleasing environment, creating an experience with no questioning of content.

24 Lyotard (1984).

25 Cf. Pinker (1994, p. 304 ff.).

26 An apparent exception to this is the case of real people speaking to each other in a simulation such as a massively multiplayer online role-playing game. The

players' actions are limited by the simulation, but their speech is not. How their words are understood, however, is heavily influenced by the context of the game.

27 The exception to this is scientific simulations which are validated by comparing their results with observations of the external universe. By submitting to this test they acknowledge a reality outside of themselves and are therefore capable of producing genuinely new knowledge. However, if, as sometimes happens, users of these simulations fail to verify and validate them at appropriate intervals, their results lose this vital contact with the external world and become effects of the simulation.

28 "[S]imulation models that break the complexity barrier almost unavoidably provide only limited understanding" (Kuorikoski, 2012, p. 180).

29 Another aspect of this is the continually shifting relationship between art and philosophy since the mid-20th Century, which has undergone periods in which art has been seen as embodying philosophical ideas, requiring its audiences to have extensive knowledge of these in order to grasp the meaning of artworks. See Danto (1986, p. iv ff.).

30 Mendelsohn (2012).

2
DRAWING AND ARCHITECTURE

What can be shown, cannot be said.

(Ludwig Wittgenstein)[1]

Drawing has played a vital role in Western architectural thought and practice since the Renaissance. Indeed, architecture, as we have known it since that time, is impossible without it. The invention of a system of drawing that permitted architects to create designs and transmit them to builders enabled the separation of design and building, the foundation of the modern practice of architecture. The centrality of drawing to architecture is now being challenged for the first time in 500 years by digital tools that create radically new relationships among architect, design, and construction. In order to understand the changes brought about by these new tools, we need some understanding of how drawing has shaped the form and substance of architectural thought and practice.

The subject of drawing in architecture is vast, but our focus will be on those aspects of drawing that will be most affected by its replacement by digital technologies. First, a particular class of drawings will be identified, within the enormous range of drawings that could be considered to be in some sense architectural, that most influence design thinking and its relationship to construction. Next, these drawings will be analyzed in order to understand how they influence architectural thought and practice. This will reveal that drawing in this sense is far more than a "medium of communication" (with the neutrality and transparency that this phrase implies); it creates the conditions for, and indeed the very possibility of, architecture as a realm of thought and activity as it has been understood for the past five centuries. This kind of architectural drawing is inseparable from design thinking, the basis of a distinct, non-discursive mode of thought. It is also a craft, a hallmark of the architect, whose exercise permits exploration of both visual and non-visual aspects of building and underlies a unique mode of understanding suited to designing spatial experience in all its complexity. Finally, as the primary medium of communication in the building industry, it shapes the roles of the various parties to a project and exerts a profound influence on building practice.

One further note before getting down to business. Some readers may wonder why the focus here is exclusively on drawing to the exclusion of physical models. Certainly models often play an important role in an architect's design process; some architects rely on them in the early stages of design. However, there are several reasons why drawing is more fundamental to the architecture of the past 500 years than models. Models are almost never used as construction documents in modern practice. Drawing, supplemented by text, bears the burden of communicating a design to constructors and therefore the properties of drawing are decisive in the relationship between design and construction. Furthermore, the effects models have on an architect's design thinking must eventually be translated into and developed through drawing. The greater abstraction of drawings makes them more flexible in mediating the ineffable gap between thought and the world of spatial experience. Whereas models usually represent only form, drawings can simultaneously represent disparate aspects of a design, crucial for allowing the designer to understand complex problems (Figure 2.1). Finally, there is a kind of homology between the act of drawing and that of laying out a building on its site. As Marco Frascari writes, "[T]he traditional design tools were analogical tools: the square used on paper to guide the tracing of lines corresponded to the square used on site to guide the erection of walls."[2] A physical connection is thus established between drawing and building bringing architects closer to the act of construction, placing their thinking in contact with the reality they are anticipating.

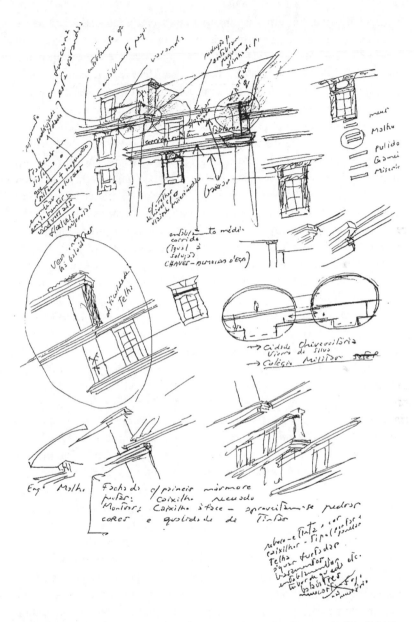

FIGURE 2.1   Alvaro Siza, sketch for the renovation of Baixa Pombalina (1995). The architect studies several details and their relationship to the façade.

Source: Image © Alvaro Siza.

Broadly speaking, any drawing that represents a piece of architecture may be considered an architectural drawing. Almost any drawing can be made architectural in this sense by framing it as a representation of a piece of architecture or an architectural idea. Here we will consider only drawings that play a role in the conception or construction of a piece of architecture, that mediate thought and construction. Such drawings span the gulf between the numinous world of the imagination and the concrete world of inhabitable structures and spaces. Anyone who has used drawings in an architectural design process knows that the relationship between ideas and drawings is complex. Mental images form from ideas whose origins are obscure or unknown. Images do not present themselves to our minds so clearly that we can simply copy them in a drawing. As more factors are added to a design problem, it becomes increasingly difficult to form clear ideas and mental images. The initial task of drawing is to give these vague ideas and images clear form. This is usually an iterative process. The first drawing will be far from adequately expressing an idea, but it is a beginning. By its definiteness, a drawing always raises questions that demand further refinement of the underlying idea. Drawing and idea gradually converge and an idea acquires form in drawings that serve as a point of departure for the design process.

The drawings at issue here have a special relationship to their referents in that they represent and generate their objects at the same time.[3] As Robin Evans puts it, this type of architectural drawing "is not so much produced by reflection on the reality outside the drawing, as *productive of a reality* that will end up outside the drawing"[4] (my italics). Prior to its representation in drawing, a design cannot be said to exist. The mental image giving rise to the representation is not a literal picture of the object; the drawing is not a copy of it. The mental image exists in a different way than the object, being perceived by the mind rather than by the eye and hand. It lacks form in the sense that tangible objects have form. Drawing brings the mental image into the visible realm, giving it tangible expression. The image can be clarified by a series of drawings representing it in different ways (Figure 2.2). Like any representation, drawings reflexively shape the ideas giving rise to them, so that the representation is a hybrid product of an idea and the properties of the representational medium. The properties of the drawing medium have a great deal to do with how architecture is created and how it emerges from thought to appear in the world.

FIGURE 2.2   Terry Dwan, *Briccola Console* (2009). The architect uses several types of drawing as well as a photograph to explore the formal, visual and material aspects of her design.

Source: Image © Terry Dwan.

Mozart claimed to be able to compose in his head and said that setting down a score was for him merely transcribing a composition that was fully formed in his mind. This is plausible because musical notation (as regards the pitch and duration of tones) has only to represent certain discrete, permitted values in Western music.[5] Forms in space are not discrete in this way. A representation of spatial form must allow for an infinite continuum of profiles and dimensions. The roughest sketch collapses the practically infinite possibilities suggested by a mental image into a restricted range defined by the general shape of the sketch. The designer will make repeated attempts to draw a form, searching for a better correspondence between his mental image and the form on the paper (Figure 2.3). Each successive mark influences the next, so that the mental image and the sketch itself both affect the sketch as it matures. The process of drawing itself thus influences its final form.

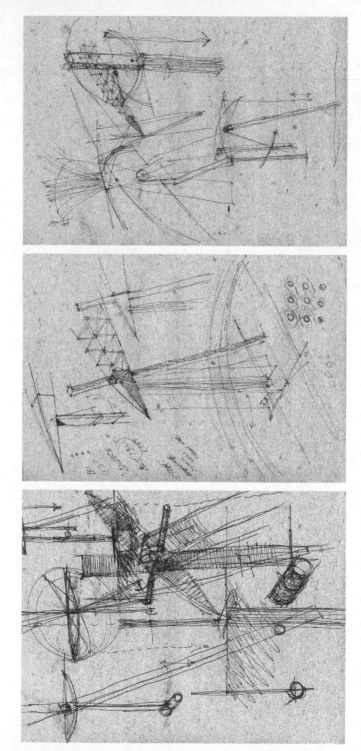

FIGURE 2.3 Wesley Taylor, three sketches from an entry for the Contraband & Freedman's Cemetery Memorial Competition (2008). A series of sketches exploring an idea of form and construction.

Source: Image © Wesley Taylor.

Drawing and Knowledge

> Drawing is a specific epistemic practice for making architectural issues
> visible and thus allows for a critical examination and debate.
>
> *(Jan Bovelet)[6]*

Drawing is not simply a medium for representing architectural ideas, but
a means of producing knowledge about architecture itself. Architectural
drawing involves definite procedures and conventions that not only make
ideas visible but also create an ideational framework for their public
evaluation and collaborative development. How we draw affects how we
think, privately and together.

If architecture represents any ideas, it does so via the medium of space.
The logic that relates architectural elements to each other is spatial, as
opposed to discursive logic, which is what we usually mean when we
refer to "logic." The latter comprises rules that govern the use of language
and concepts that ensure the intelligibility and coherence of linguistic
propositions. Spatial logic, on the other hand, is aconceptual. It applies
to relationships of form, scale, and juxtaposition that produce coherent
spatial arrangements. While architectural elements have names and thus
associated concepts, it is the spatial relationships among these elements
that create architectural experience. An architectural composition can be
described verbally (e.g. "the column stands on a plinth and supports a
lintel") but this hardly describes the experience of being in its presence.
A concept like "support" is too broad to evoke the precise manner in
which the lintel rests on the column. However much detail is added to
the verbal description, it will never approach the specific, instantaneous
understanding produced by experience (Figure 2.4).

The relationships of spatial logic are understood visually. Diagrams
and graphs are good examples of this. A graph translates various types of
data into spatial relationships and can reveal order in them that a list
of numbers does not (Figure 2.5). Diagrams spatialize information that
may not be spatial in nature (Figure 2.6, p. 57). In this example, the
drawn shapes represent various groups of people with an interest in
a project. The diagram expresses the idea that while each group has a
different set of concerns about the project, these overlap in a certain area
and that this defines the design problem. Although the idea conveyed in
the diagram can be approximated in words (as I just did), the diagram is
more specific and contains less extraneous information. Paradoxically, by

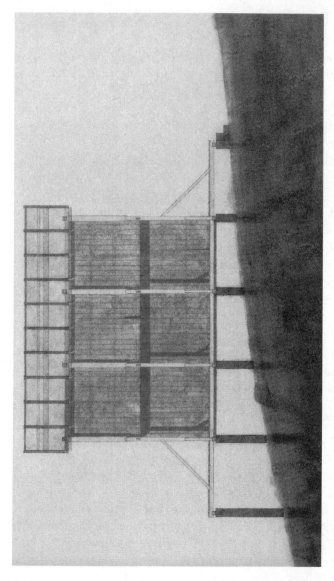

FIGURE 2.4 Walter Pichler, *House for the Birds, side view* (1978). The architect is very precise about all the connections in the project, particularly the way the building and the platform rest on the piles. The character of the design is largely found in these details.

Source: Image courtesy Anna Triphamer.

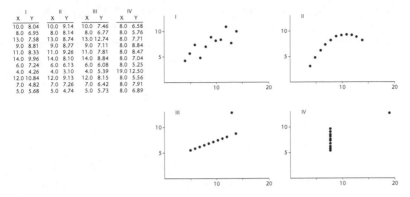

FIGURE 2.5 The four sets of data in the table at left are graphed at right. The order in the data is immediately apparent when they are displayed visually.

Source: Graphics Press.

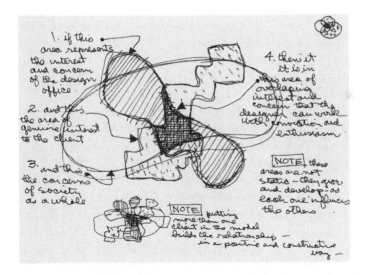

FIGURE 2.6 Charles Eames, design diagram. The various parties to a project are represented by intersecting shapes. The diagram communicates the idea that the project lies at the intersection of the interests of these groups without specifying any extraneous information about what those interests are or what constitutes a group. The diagram embodies the pure idea of separate entities and their commonalities, providing a general description that applies to many aspects of the project.

Source: © 2013 Eames Office LLC (eamesoffice.com).

being vague about exactly what these shapes represent (their content), the diagram is more specific than its verbal translation. Drawing embodies spatial logic and thus contributes to our knowledge in a way other representations cannot.[7] Making a mark on a sheet of paper converts a featureless, homogeneous surface into a differentiated two-dimensional space by providing a point of reference by which any future marks can be located (it is not for nothing that we use the phrase "to draw a distinction"). By creating spatial knowledge, drawing adds an entirely new dimension to our understanding. Its ability to spatialize many kinds of ideas allows it to represent disparate kinds of ideas on the same surface, providing a means to study and synthesize many aspects of a building design. The common basis of drawing and architecture in spatial logic accounts for drawing's unique ability to convey architectural ideas.

While the two-dimensional nature of drawing may appear at first to pose a problem for representing three-dimensional reality, it is in fact a great advantage. Our experience of buildings is *diachronic* (i.e. it takes place over time) while a drawing is *synchronic*, meaning that it does not change with time. Drawing captures our diachronic experience in a series of synchronic representations, allowing us to study and discuss the spatial relationships it expresses. Drawing is thus essential to both public discourse about architecture and the development of the architect's thinking.[8]

Architectural ideas originate in the mind of an individual designer whose drawings may be hermetic and meaningful only to her. As a means of incorporating non-spatial ideas into a design, such drawings often represent many things in addition to ideas about built form. They may even have no obvious reference to it (Figures 2.7, 2.8). Eventually, however, the process must become public in order to involve others, and such drawings must give way to other drawings that are clear to other people and allow them to contribute to the design. At that moment architectural drawing takes on certain aspects of language in that it permits communication through the use of conventions. In creating its conventions, architecture follows a pattern found in science in which each discipline develops its own technical terminology.[9] Architecture is not a science, but if it is to generate knowledge it needs drawing conventions for the same reason that science needs its terminology, which is to permit discourse and knowledge sharing.[10]

Conventions are normally arbitrary, but many drawing conventions may not appear so at first, since they resemble the form of the building

FIGURE 2.7 Svein Tonsager, three drawings from the series *Inner Spaces* (1996). The relationship of these drawings to architecture lies in the exploration of the spatial idea of *interior*. The compositions explore different ways interior space can be defined and its relationships to an exterior that serves as its foil. The architect may or may not be exploring a formal vocabulary for building as well.

Source: Image courtesy Annette Brunsvig Sorensen.

FIGURE 2.8 Hyun Joo Lee, *Layers in Knot* (2013). A complex interweaving of representational and pictorial space is created by manipulating conventions of overlay and transparency. The drawing explores its dual status as representation and object.

Source: Image © Hyun Joo Lee.

elements they describe. A floor plan, for example, can easily be related to the layout of a building, as an elevation can to its appearance. However, even these aspects of drawing are based on conventions specifically created for the purpose of communicating a building's design. Although an elevation drawn by a Renaissance architect looks very similar to one drawn today, they are in fact based on two very different conventions. The similarity exists due to a "happy marriage of style and drawing in the Classical order."[11] Because Renaissance building forms were based on models of Antiquity, their forms were frontal, prismatic, and generally bilaterally symmetric (Figure 2.9). Their representation in drawing could therefore be thought of in terms of preserving proportions and angles, with no geometrically consistent idea of projection.[12] Modern orthographic drawings are mathematically-based projections (Figure 2.10). If a building happens to be frontal and prismatic, the results are very similar to Renaissance plans and elevations. Buildings need not have these qualities to be portrayed accurately by modern projections which can describe a much larger variety of forms.

Thus what appear to be natural signs can be conventions in disguise. Conventions can serve an ideological function if their assumptions are reified, masking their arbitrary nature. Thoughtful architects need to be alive to this possibility and question their representational methods to discern and challenge hidden assumptions. In this way, conventions can

FIGURE 2.9
Andrea Palladio, Villa Emo (1559). The Renaissance assumptions of symmetry and frontality in building form were embodied in the drawing conventions of the time that have persisted to our day.

Source: Mhwater/GFDL.

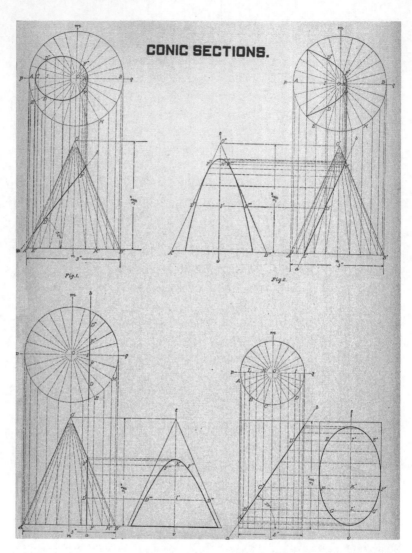

FIGURE 2.10 Conic sections: exercises in descriptive geometry. From *A Textbook of Architectural Drawing* (Scranton, PA: International Correspondence Schools, 1901). Descriptive geometry generates any view of an object from other views. The position of the viewer with respect to the object is no longer assumed to be frontal and the object itself need not be symmetrical to be accurately described in drawing.

indirectly produce knowledge. By critically examining drawing, hitherto unrecognized assumptions and prejudices in architectural thinking can be revealed. One obvious such prejudice is the priority given to the visual aspect of architecture by drawing. It would be more accurate to say that drawing privileges architecture's *visualizable* aspects, since drawing can represent non-visual ideas. Yet this is also to some extent the result of conventions. Privately, an architect can represent almost any aspect of a building in drawing. Publicly, however, there are few conventions that allow the expression of non-visual dimensions of experience.

Geometry

> [G]eometric forms move easily across the border between the visible and the invisible, the corporeal and the incorporeal, the absolute and the contingent, the ideal and the real.
>
> *(Robin Evans)[13]*

In different guises, geometry inhabits both the world of thought and that of physical reality, providing crucial links between them. We can draw a form such as a triangle and thus bring it into sensible reality, allowing it to become an element in a design, for example. But any drawing has features that are not part of our *idea* of a triangle, which consists abstractly of three sides and three angles. Yet a drawing does not distort the idea. The features of the drawn triangle that depart from the ideal somehow vanish and we are in contact with the ideal as we look at the drawing.

What is the connection between an ideal and a drawing that permits this remarkable identification? Kant suggested that mediating the ideal and visible forms there is a mental image of the form. He saw this as a kind of mental drawing: "I cannot represent to myself a line, however small, without drawing it in thought, that is, generating from a point all its parts one after another."[14] In this account, a mental image is generated by an imaginative process analogous to drawing, starting at one point and tracing the form from that point. This is very different than the usual process of representation in which the relationship between the visible signifier and its mental signified is arbitrary and conventional. In geometry, the relationship between signifier and signified is not arbitrary. The signified here is the mental image; the drawing, created by a process similar to that which created the image in the first place, evokes the signified in a natural rather than conventional manner. If Kant is right that the mental image of a geometric shape is a process rather than a fixed thing, then a drawing is not a representation of a pre-existing shape in the mind. The process of creating the mental image must be repeated every time the image is summoned. Only when it is committed to paper or some other physical medium does it become a synchronous object that can be grasped as a whole and studied at length. This account is useful in helping us understand the unique role of geometry in drawing and architecture based on it. By describing the mental image as a process analogous to drawing, Kant makes his account explicitly two-dimensional. It is apparent that there is no such naturalness in drawing three-dimensional objects, evidenced by the many different ways this has been done throughout history. If drawing is to represent three dimensions by two, it must make use of conventions.

As Robin Evans describes at length in his essential book, *The Projective Cast*, the meaning of geometry in architecture has changed markedly over time. Evans identifies three types of geometry that have been implicit in architecture at different times: metrical, projective and symbolic.[15] Each of these reflected the conception of space prevalent at the time, and architectural design both expressed this conception and was conditioned by it. Metrical geometry is concerned with the absolute measure of objects and therefore operates in a static, universal Euclidean space. Projective geometry addresses the appearance of objects which depends on the position from which they are seen. Its central operation is transformation, specifically the transformation of one view of an object into another. Both metric and projective geometry are closely tied to drawing and graphical representation. In the metrical case, a scaled-down but otherwise isomorphic copy of a two-dimensional geometric figure is recorded on a sheet of paper. In the case of projection, a transformation from one view to another is constructed graphically by reflection and rotation (Figure 2.10). Both can be regarded as graphical proofs of the geometric consistency (and therefore the spatial possibility) of an object or a design. A metrical drawing demonstrates how a building is to be laid out using a simple transformation: scale. The consistency of this transformation, proved by Euclid, ensures that the building can be laid out according to the drawing. A projective drawing proves that two representations describe one and the same object.

Ideal or Platonic forms have played a unique role in architecture, appearing over and over again in the architectures of many cultures and times (Figures 2.11, 2.12, 2.13).The clarity of our mental image of these forms sets them apart in the realm of visual experience. Renaissance thought attributed the special quality of these forms to the common divine origin of the order of the world and human understanding. Modern architects have found their esthetic value in their relationship to forms of thought. In advocating architectural composition based on these forms, Le Corbusier identified beauty with the clarity with which the mind apprehends such forms.[16] The clarity of our mental image of these forms results from their high degree of symmetry which permits us to grasp them in their entirety from a single point of view. Symmetry links vision with comprehension; thus, beauty for Le Corbusier originates in an association of sensory experience with intellectual comprehension, a congruence of sensory experience and thought. In both cases, the notion of ideal architectural form is grounded in an association between visual experience and intellectual comprehension, of visible form with forms in the Platonic sense of Ideas.

Like all ideas, geometric forms must arise from our sensory experience. Being concerned with measurement, Euclidean geometry is rooted in our bodies, our fundamental measure of space. When it comes to objects in space, our primary sense is tactile. Maurice Merleau-Ponty and others have suggested that our ability to recognize form visually is rooted in our sense of touch, that we learn about forms by handling them and transfer this experience to vision. How do we derive ideal geometric forms from our experience? We find among certain families of shapes

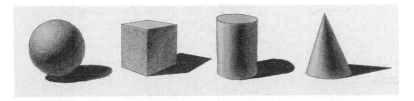

FIGURE 2.11 The Platonic solids were valued for their symbolism by the Renaissance and for their perceptual clarity by Modernists such as Le Corbusier.

Source: CC BY 2.0.

FIGURE 2.12
The Stupa
of Buddha's
disciple, Sanchi,
Madya Pradesh,
India.

Source: Raveesh
Vyas/CC BY-SA
2.0.

FIGURE 2.13
Portable market
hut, Mbabane,
Swaziland.

Source: Photo by
John Atherton

similarities which allow us to project from them "limit" forms that embody their commonalities[17] (Figure 2.14). This impulse to idealize the forms of everyday objects emerges in early childhood, as evidenced by children's drawings featuring circular heads and houses composed of a triangle sitting atop a square (Figure 2.15). The operations of Euclidean geometry are thus experiential as well as abstract, taking place simultaneously on the tactile, visual, and intellectual planes. This type of geometry is the nexus of the mind and the physical universe.

From the 15th through the 17th Century, the prevalent spatial conception in western Europe was Euclidean. This space has no inherent structure; it is "eternal and indestructible, [providing] a position for everything that comes to be."[18] It is structured by the forms placed within it. By their presence, primary geometric forms create spatial hierarchies based on centers and axes. It also gives proportions great significance, as these allow an object to develop according to a measure that arises from within itself. This led to prismatic architectural forms which lent themselves well to description by linear perspective in which parallel planes were essential.

Euclidean geometry allows the transposition of spatial ideas into visible, measurable form and back again. It establishes a clear relationship between architectural drawings and construction, avoiding the necessity of specifying the location of each point individually. Euclidean theorems are everywhere, ensuring the construction of equal angles, parallel lines, equal lengths and definite proportions. Many of these theorems depend on the properties of the circle, which Euclid includes among his Definitions that underlie his entire system. The process of drawing in this mode directly prefigures the layout of the building on the site. The builder reconstructs the plan drawn by the architect by reproducing the geometry of the drawing on the site, making use of Euclid's above-mentioned theorems. These requirements impose practical limitations on the variety

FIGURE 2.14 The prairie crocus. Nature reveals geometry.

Source: Photo © Martin van den Akker.

FIGURE 2.15 Drawing of his dream house by Thato, age 7, Lonely Park Township, Mafikeng, South Africa. Euclidean forms appear in children's drawings from many places and cultures. The origins of this image of a house are another matter.

Source: Image courtesy of artist and SOS Africa.

of forms that can be used in building designs. In principle, any form can be drawn and reproduced in the field; in practice, forms that exceed some level of complexity (i.e. some degree of deviance from simple Euclidean forms) are difficult to draw (and even more difficult to build) and so are effectively excluded from the building vocabulary. Such practical limitations on building form were not experienced as such by architects until rather recently. The theories that had underwritten design practice since the Renaissance were founded upon Euclidean space which served to unite the divine/ideal with the tangible/pragmatic. Theoretical, esthetic and practical considerations converged in the Euclidean notion of space.

Beginning in the late 17th Century, the Euclidean idea of space was supplanted by Cartesian space, a neutral, descriptive framework, the purpose of which is to specify the location of objects. Unlike Euclidean space, it has an inherent structure, usually pictured as an infinitely divisible grid of points specified by three numbers (Figure 2.16). Placing an object such as a building in this space does not impose an order on it. On the contrary, the structure of the space imposes its order on the building (Figure 2.17). The centers, axes, and so on created by objects in this space have no absolute significance as they do in Euclidean space. In the

Euclidean case, the object is the generator of space; its center becomes the center of space itself. This allowed Renaissance and Baroque churches to establish an *axis mundi*, to symbolize a universe understood as having an absolute center. By contrast, Cartesian space has no center or any other absolute position (an idea Isaac Newton rejected as irreligious even though his theories required it); the location of every point within it is only determined relatively to others. The center (now called the origin) is chosen by the observer and can be changed at will to suit his purposes. This conception of space gave rise to a consistent understanding of projection in architectural drawing. Whereas Renaissance drawing had been concerned with giving true measure from a single ideal vantage point, drawing now became capable of transforming the appearance of an object from one point of view to another. The axial, infinitely distant viewpoint no longer had special significance and building designs eventually came to reflect the absence of privileged viewpoints. This emphasis on transformation as the key operation in architectural drawing emerged from the practice of *traits* in stereotomy, drawings which showed how to

FIGURE 2.16 The most common representation of Cartesian space: an infinite grid without a center. It serves only to locate points within it, lending significance to none.

Source: Author.

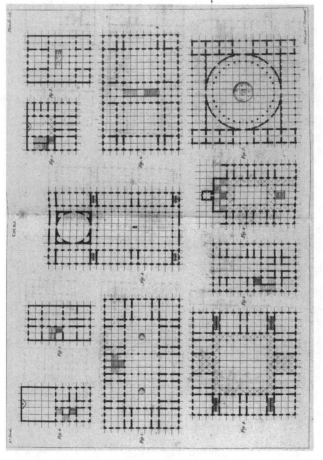

FIGURE 2.17 J-N-L. Durand, Plate 15 from the *Précis des leçons d'architecture données à l'École royale polytechnique* (1802 or 1809). With the deployment of Cartesian space in architecture, the regular module replaced the system of proportions that unified Renaissance buildings.

Source: Rare Books Division, Special Collections, J. Willard Marriott Library, University of Utah.

FIGURE 2.18 Le Corbusier, Chapel of Nôtre Dame du Haut, Ronchamp (c. 1954). Instrumentalized gometry. An enigmatic form whose meaning has been debated since its completion. Whatever it may be, it is unlikely to derive from the descriptive geometry that was used to build it.

Source: Photo by Sandra Cohen-Rose and Colin Rose.

FIGURE 2.19 Le Corbusier, Chapel of Nôtre Dame du Haut, Ronchamp, Sketch (1957). This sketch, made by Le Corbusier from the completed building, indicates what he saw in his finished work. Compare Figure 2.24.

Source: © 2013 Artists Rights Society (ARS), New York/ADAGP, Paris/F.L.C.

carve complicated pieces of stone masonry. This approach was finally systematized by Gaspard Monge in his *Descriptive Geometry* of 1799.

In architecture, descriptive geometry made possible the design and construction of a much wider range of forms. Buildings did not begin to take full advantage of this freedom until materials (steel and reinforced concrete) became available that permitted the realization of complex forms. The design of buildings like Nôtre Dame du Haut (Figures 2.18, 2.19) was only possible through descriptive geometry. Meaning is no longer immanent in geometry; it has devolved into an instrument for describing form. For example, the geometry of the form of the roof of Nôtre Dame du Haut is based on a class of forms called ruled surfaces. This was essential to its designers as a descriptive tool, but it is not the ideal origin of the form as was the circle in a centralized church. The significance of this form has been the subject of much speculation, but no one thinks that it lies in the fact that it can be described by ruled surfaces.

Drawing as Craft

> The laborer with a sense of craft becomes engaged in the work in and for itself; the satisfactions of working are their own reward.
>
> *(C. Wright Mills)*[19]

So far, our discussion of drawing and architecture has concerned its more abstract aspects. Now we will consider it as a physical activity, a craft within the larger craft of architecture. Craftsmanship entails a special state of mind on the part of the craftsman. What distinguishes the craftsman from other workers is the engagement of the former with the task at hand. The craftsman is motivated by the goal of producing high quality work for its own sake rather than for an external reward. This is a good thing in all types of work, but it is essential in architecture. No incentive other than love of the work itself can elicit the degree of care and personal involvement that architects invest in their work. An architect's work is always a gift in the sense that it is created out of a personal concern that has no price.

The craft of drawing has been fundamental to architectural craft and a major constituent of the architect's professional identity. Achieving mastery of drawing has traditionally been an important phase in the architect's training, a rite of passage in becoming a member of the community of architects. Belonging to this community provides critical social support for architects in their daily work and reaffirms their commitment to doing good work for its own sake. Mastery of drawing, like the mastery of any craft, is achieved by repetitive practice,[20] which in this case trains the mind, eye, and hand to work seamlessly together. The unification of these three faculties is fundamental to the cognitive functions of drawing described above. With practice, the hand learns to perform a repertoire of gestures without conscious guidance, so that it seems to have a mind of its own. For a master of this craft, a drawing seems to be a product of a nearly transparent connection between the imagination and the hand.

Repetition itself is a key to the efficacy of drawing as a cognitive tool. Going over a drawing many times affords the architect the opportunity to experiment, to search for the proper expression of an idea, critically examine the work and generate new ideas. This teaches the architect to value the process itself as a search for ideas and expression, keeping an open mind and tolerating the uncertainty and vagueness it involves (Figure 2.20). Vagueness in an early drawing is a virtue: it shows the true state of the project in the designer's mind, avoiding implying knowledge where none exists. As Juhani Pallasmaa writes, "A sense of certainty, satisfaction and finality that arises too early in the [design] process can be catastrophic."[21] Focus on process rather than the state of a project at a moment in time is essential if the project is to be capable of discovery, or anything beyond the mere will of its designer. It allows the project to

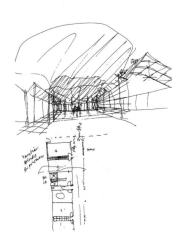

FIGURE 2.20 Glenn Murcutt, house for an Aboriginal community, sketch section and plan (1992–94). The architect leaves the shape and structure of the roof vague as he investigates the spatial qualities of a long narrow space.

Source: Glenn Murcutt, Courtesy Architecture Foundation Australia.

"speak" to the designer, maintaining the architect in a receptive state of mind necessary to remain alive to the complex of forces acting on the design and alert to the new possibilities they raise. This in turn allows architects to reach beyond their current state of knowledge and use new knowledge to inform the design.

The crucial involvement of the hand in drawing shows it to be an activity that requires the engagement of the body. Our bodies are not mere vessels that carry our brains and sensory organs around; they are the basic condition of our experience and therefore of our thought. Our very notion of space may originate in our experience of our bodies: in assembling a single, unified body image from our awareness of its parts, space may arise as the medium in which relationships among them exist.[22] Our experience is therefore not objective or disinterested, but always in the context of our place within the world. Henri Matisse said, "A drawing of a tree shows, not a tree, but a tree-being-looked-at."[23]

Our experience of buildings, like all of our experience, is through our bodies, although in Western culture we have emphasized its visual aspects.[24] The origin of architectural ideas is not purely intellectual or visual, but also *haptic*, i.e. emanating from our embodied perception. Pallasmaa believes that "[a]rchitectural ideas arise 'biologically' from unconceptualized and lived existential knowledge rather than from mere analyses and intellect."[25] The hand, as the primary organ of touch, provides this aconceptual body-knowledge. It has been suggested that vision, which our culture has elevated above the other senses, is in fact rooted in our sense of touch. In this view, seeing is, as it were, touch at a distance; our understanding of form originates in our hands as we literally or imaginatively hold objects and feel their shapes.[26] Drawing provides a means of thinking in this mode. Through the hand, drawing re-establishes the body as the seat of experience and restores to vision its tactile nature. Drawing affords the designer a medium that permits—requires—connections among hand (body), mind, and eye that create our experience of the world.

In some form, the experience of making a drawing is present in the drawing itself. Looking at a drawing often evokes the process that created it. The viewer experiences the drawing, not just as a visual image, but as a made *thing* that emerged from someone's hand, embodying their ideas and intentions. The specific qualities of the linework or shading that are products of the individual designer's sensibility evoke a sympathetic

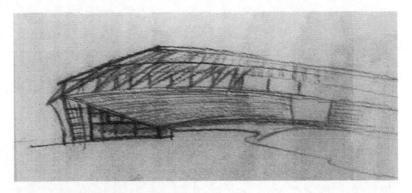

FIGURE 2.21   Aarti Kathuria, stadium roof sketch (2013). The strong gestures in this sketch allow the viewer to feel the motion of the designer's hand.

Source: Image © Aarti Kathuria.

response in the viewer who is placed in intimate contact with the experience of the designer, almost taking the designer's place (Figure 2.21). Most designers have a distinctive manner of drawing and certain preferred media that are as individual as handwriting and are uniquely suited to the expression of the aspects of architecture that most interest them (Figures 2.22, 2.23). An architect's manner of drawing and design predilections influence each other, as do drawing and design in general (Figure 2.24).

The qualities of drawing media have profound effects on the experience of drawing and thereby on the architect's design process and the building being designed. Like all materials, drawing media have innate qualities that must be understood before they can be used to express a designer's intentions. The understanding of these qualities resides in the body. It is useless to talk about the qualities of different papers; they must be felt, handled and drawn upon with different media. Through this tactile experience, the hand comes to understand the paper and the action of media upon it. At the same time, the eyes have been active in assessing the visual results of various combinations of paper and media such as inks, pencils, charcoal, or washes. Only when this understanding has been achieved can an architect choose the right combination of media to realize his intentions in a drawing. The choice of media is a crucial part of any drawing. The chosen media have a profound influence on the drawing and the final result is in some way the child of the designer's intentions and the qualities of the media. With experience, the architect learns to

FIGURES 2.22 AND 2.23 Aldo Rossi, *Marseille* (1993) and Aldo Rossi, *Il Duomo di Milano* (1982). Rossi's frequent use of line and shadow simplifies form to allow him to study the urban ensembles which were the focus of his research and design practice.

Source: Image courtesy Fondazione Aldo Rossi, Milan.

FIGURE 2.24 Le Corbusier, travel sketches (Athens, Pompeii, Pisa). In these early sketches, Le Corbusier shows his concerns for plans, which are drawn in thin lines, and volumes, which are drawn in shaded perspective to reveal their visual effects.

Source: © 2013 Artists Rights Society (ARS), New York/ADAGP, Paris/F.L.C.

account for and take advantage of these qualities so that their intentions are in part shaped by them, influencing their thinking (Figures 2.25, 2.26). This experience is similar to that of a woodworker who takes the qualities of a piece of wood into account when designing a piece of furniture. It gives architects an experience with how materials and intentions interact to shape a design, a crucial understanding they will apply in their design thinking.

Mastering drawing entails mastery of its tools. With sufficient practice, these tools become extensions of the architect's hands and manipulating a tool is experienced simply as moving the hand. All that has been said above about the haptic nature of drawing takes place through tools. Naturally, it is not the hand itself that draws, but a tool manipulated by the hand. When we say that the hand learns gestures and so forth, what we really mean is that the hand–tool combination does so. Tools are associated with a medium and are designed to act upon that medium in specific ways. Tools are thus a means of understanding a medium: we learn about the material world through their use. They provide feedback through the hand and thereby the body; it is this that actually provides the haptic dimension of drawing.

The tools of drawing stimulate the architect's thinking. In his book *The Craftsman*, Richard Sennett describes how tools teach us about the world. He distinguishes between two types: "fit-for-purpose" and "multi-purpose" tools. The former, being designed to perform a single task, make their use obvious, as a t-square is made for drawing straight lines. Multi-purpose tools are open-ended and challenge their users by their very lack of specificity:

> Getting better at using tools comes to us, in part, when the tools challenge us, and this challenge often occurs just because the tools are not fit-for-purpose. They may not be good enough, or it's hard to figure out how to use them. The challenge becomes greater when we are obliged to use these tools to repair or undo mistakes. In both creation and repair, the challenge can be met by adapting the form of a tool, or improvising with it as it is, using it in ways it was not meant for. However we come to use it, the very incompleteness of the tool has taught us something.[27]

The best example of this among drawing tools is the pencil. A pencil can make an enormous variety of marks and, due to its sensitivity to orientation and pressure, it can transmit extremely subtle hand movements to the paper. Yet it may happen that a pencil is not "good enough" in Sennett's sense. A draftsman may try to "improve" it by trying different techniques, holding it or shaping the point differently, experimenting with pencils of different hardness or different types of paper. They may be led to consider the pencil in its generality as something that makes marks on paper, and open their search to other kinds of drawing instruments or media. The multiplicity of a pencil's uses is a challenge and opportunity to learn about our ideas as we try to express them more clearly by experimenting with the tool.

Sennett's reference to "repair" is also important in the context of drawing. Again, if we understand the function of a drawing to be the expression and development of ideas, a drawing can be considered broken

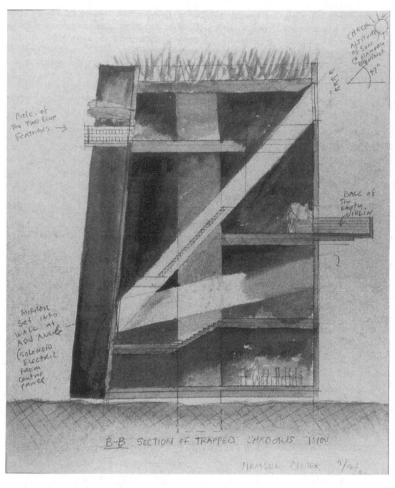

FIGURES 2.25 AND 2.26 Steven Holl, conceptual sketches (section and elevation) for the Knut Hamsun Center (1996). Holl's use of watercolor here evinces an interest in large surfaces characterized by their overall shape and variation in texture. The technique also forces a certain intentional clunkiness, refusing refinement to all parts of the construction. It also lends itself to dramatic representations of light.

Source: Image ©Steven Holl.

if it does not express an idea to the designer's satisfaction. They may simply start over, or they may try to "repair" the drawing by making changes to it. In the latter case they will look for parts of the drawing that don't "work" (don't express their intentions well), replace or augment them with different marks and evaluate the result. In this process the designer learns both about the drawing and the ideas behind it, since a failure of the drawing could be due to the drawing itself, a lack of clarity in the ideas, or both. They will learn about both how the drawing responds to the designer's ideas and how their thinking motivates the drawing. The designer is being pushed forward by a sense that there is something more the drawing can do.

This epistemic function of tools is one of the primary issues to consider in thinking about the consequences of replacing manual drawing with digital tools. At first glance, computers seem to lack many of the characteristics of drawing that has made it so fundamental for architectural design. They appear not to engage our bodies in anything like the way drawing does. Moving a mouse is extremely crude compared with handling a pencil, and utterly lacking in tactile feedback. A pressure-sensitive digital drawing tablet is an improvement, but the tactile feedback it provides is extremely limited compared with that provided by a pencil on paper. Furthermore, both involve a disjunction between the hand and the eye: the hand is on the desk while the eye is on a monitor. Compare this with how the eye follows and guides the motion of the hand in drawing. It should now be clear that the oft-heard cliché that "the computer is just another pencil" is categorically untrue. The question is whether we want computers to act like pencils (a matter of their interface perhaps) or view them as an entirely different type of tool that manifests and guides our thought in radically different ways.

Pleasure

The act of drawing can be very pleasurable. Small children almost universally seem to take to it with gusto. This enjoyment is experienced by many who draw without questioning its source, but it is important to ask why drawing is so enjoyable. For the proficient, it provides the always-enjoyable experience of exercising a well-honed skill. But even for the novice, there is something about drawing that verges on compulsion: give someone a pencil and a sheet of paper and chances are they will draw, if only a "doodle."[28] There is something deep at work here.

One possibility is that drawing heals the culturally imposed separation between mind and body. The coordinated activity of the eye, mind, and hand produces a total engagement that absorbs both intellectual and haptic faculties, unifying mind and body much as playing a musical instrument does. In drawing, the pre-eminence given to vision in Western culture is replaced by an integration of vision with the tactile sense and with the body, allowing a perception that more closely mirrors our actual experience of the world. It helps the person drawing to return to a more natural, integrated state in which the haptic assumes its rightful, central place in our experience.

Another possibility, not at odds with the first, is that the very abstraction of drawing is pleasing. Drawing brings ideas and material together. The mind deals in abstractions; they are its working material, so to speak. It strives to understand the material world, which is a series of isolated experiences until the mind gives them some order by abstracting relationships among them. The rapprochement of the world-as-given and human comprehension is inherently pleasurable because it lends coherence to our experience, rendering the world less alien and more intelligible. If the drawing is of an existing object, it brings the brute reality of the object within our understanding. If the drawing is of something that does not yet exist, it provides the satisfaction of generating a tangible object from an abstract idea. Drawing is, in a sense, architecture writ small: it is the expression of thought and emotion by manipulating material, imbuing the inanimate world with meaning.

Whatever the case, drawing engages something profound within us, gratifies a deeply rooted need. Some writers have described this need as *cosmopoiesis*, or world-making. Such a world of our own making is a response to the world as we find it, a thought-experiment[29] seeking other possibilities more in keeping with our desires, or simply an answer to the question, "What if?" This is a way of learning, by posing what logicians call a counterfactual: asking what would happen if something that is not now the case became true. It gets us to think both about the way things are and the way they could be, a questioning of current reality by way of the imaginative creation of a different reality. This creative imagination is present in all human activities, a fundamental human trait. Drawing gives imagination immediacy, engaging the full range of our faculties as perhaps no other medium can do.

Drawing Frames Architectural Discourse

We saw above the essential role of drawing in allowing architectural discourse, the public discussion of architecture. Without such discourse, architecture, or any other creative enterprise, would not exist as a social or cultural force. Creative work remains a strictly private affair until it engages other people. Architectural discourse involves two principal kinds of questions. The first involves internal reflection, various forms of the question, "What is architecture?": its purpose, nature, proper goals, place in human life, and so on. In this vein, architects discuss such matters as dwelling and representation (Figures 2.27, 2.28). The second addresses architecture's role in society and culture. This raises such questions as how architecture represents institutions, whom it serves and its responsibilities to various constituencies. These two types of questions are not entirely distinct. For example, one must have an idea of how architecture represents in general in order to think about how to represent a specific institution (Figure 2.29).

The drawing conventions that are vital to discourse evolve to serve the needs of a particular time and place. This can be seen in the example given above of the specificity of Renaissance drawing to the accepted formal vocabulary of architecture of that period. The limitations of these

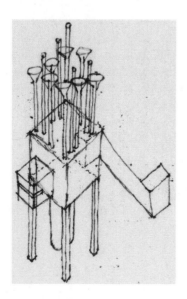

FIGURE 2.27 John Hejduk: "Widow's House" from *Lancaster-Hanover Mask* (1980–82). The occupant Hejduk specifies for this house is a social archetype: a woman's social position changes with the death of her husband. Her condition evokes loss, loneliness, incompleteness. The form is to be interpreted as an expression and questioning of this social condition.

Source: John Hejduk, fonds Collection Centre Canadien d'Architecture/Canadian Centre for Architecture, Montréal.

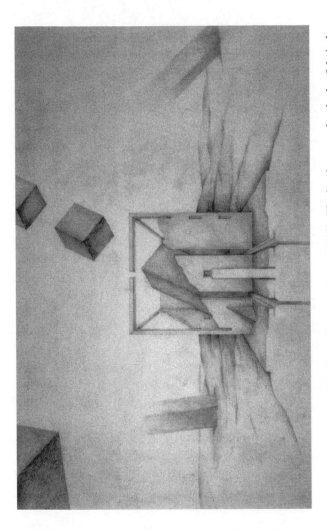

FIGURE 2.28 Raimund Abraham, *The Last House* (1983). The last house: why the last? Is it the house of the last living person? Have houses become obsolete? Is it some individual's final earthly residence? Does the architect know it is the last house he will design? In every case, the house is problematized and takes on different meanings.

Source: Image courtesy Una Abaham.

FIGURE 2.29
Philip Johnson &
John Burgee, Sony
Tower (formerly
AT&T Building,
c. 1984). Johnson's
design challenged
Modernist orthodoxy
by creating a strong
figure in the city's
skyline and providing
a distinctive image
for the corporation it
represented.

Source: Photo by David
Shankbone.

conventions were hidden from architects at the time because they complemented their ideas of architectural form and the use of drawings in construction. When ideas about design began to change, drawing conventions had to be revealed as such so that drawing could evolve to serve new ideas. A striking example of this was the acceptance of perspective in architectural representation. Alberti, who in another context had written extensively on perspective, believed that it should not be used by architects whose drawings needed to convey the true proportions of the buildings they designed.[30] The ideas of an Enlightenment architect like Etienne-Louis Boullée involved the psychological impact of scale on the viewer which could only be conveyed in perspective drawings (Figure 2.30). Perspective needed to be included among drawing conventions in order to express ideas current at the time. This process has been repeated again and again: drawing conventions first serving architectural discourse, then limiting it, and finally being overturned as architectural ideas evolve.

Conventions are essential for drawings to communicate, but they are also hiding places for unstated assumptions and ideologies. A critical examination of drawing's conventions is therefore an important aspect of architectural discourse (Figure 2.31). Drawing itself can become a tool for revealing conventions for what they are: a set of often unacknowledged assumptions that embed ideas in design, making them seem natural and inevitable when in fact they channel thinking in certain directions. So intimate is the relationship between drawing conventions and architectural thought that challenging conventions can become a means of thinking about architecture (Figure 2.32). Drawing can *become* architecture in certain circumstances, especially when the ideas being proposed render the realization of a project impossible. Such "paper architecture" has played a vital role in architectural discourse. There is a rich history of unbuilt projects that have had a deep influence on architectural thought, from Dinocrates's city carved from Mt. Athos (described by Vitruvius), to Leonardo's series of centralized church designs (Figure 2.33), the unbuilt (and in many cases unbuildable) projects of Boullée (Figure 2.30), Mies's charcoal images of glass skyscrapers (Figure 1.4) and the polemical projects of late-20th-Century architects like John Hejduk (Figure 2.34).

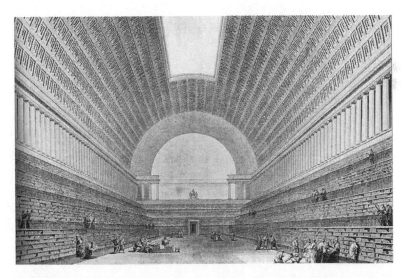

FIGURE 2.30 Etienne-Louis Boullée, project for the French National Library (1785). Boullée's ideas revolved around evoking strong emotions in the viewers. Overwhelming scale was a device he often employed. For an interior such as this, perspective was an essential tool.

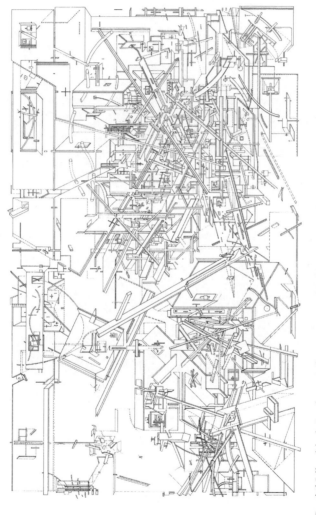

FIGURE 2.31 Daniel Libeskind, *Leakage*, Micromegas series (1979). Exploiting the conventions of axonometric drawing, Libeskind creates disorienting spaces. Objects in axonometric projection do not diminish as they recede, but Libeskind uses the simple device of reducing their size to play upon the viewer's experience of perspective and create a false sense of depth. By manipulating conventions of drawing, Libeskind reveals their conventional nature.

Source: *Leakage*, Micromegas series,© Daniel Libeskind, 1979.

FIGURE 2.32 Vladimir Krinsky, *Communal House* (1920), collection of the Museum of Modern Art, New York. Using the visual language of Cubism in an architectural drawing creates pictorial spatial ambiguity and disrupts the conventional relationship between drawing and building.

Source: Digital Image © The Museum of Modern Art/Licensed by SCALA/Art Resource, NY.

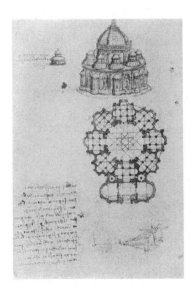

FIGURE 2.33 Leonardo da Vinci, sketches of a centrally planned church (ca. 1488). One of a series of designs by Leonardo for centrally planned churches.

FIGURE 2.34 John Hejduk, "Reaper's House" (1980–82). The "Reaper" is not as clear as the "Widow" (Figure 2.27) as a social type. The term has two senses, one benign (a reaper of crops) and one sinister (a reaper of souls; the Grim Reaper). Hejduk is playing on this ambiguity. The form is reminiscent of a windmill, but its menacing blades and internal pendulum give it the aspect of a torture chamber.

Source: John Hejduk, fonds Collection Centre Canadien d'Architecture/Canadian Centre for Architecture, Montréal.

Drawing Structures Architectural Practice

Architectural drawing evolved as the chief means of communicating the architect's ideas to builders. The authority of the architect in this paradigm was rooted in the Humanist assumption of the superiority of theoretical over practical knowledge. The Renaissance architect's primary role was to determine the form of the building and his drawings showed only this (Figure 2.35). The efficacy of these drawings depended on two practical conditions. One was the traditional nature of building

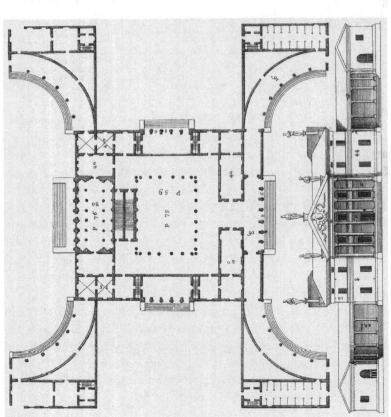

FIGURE 2.35 Andrea Palladio, Plate LVIII, Book 2 of the *Four Books of Architecture* (Villa Mocenico).

Source: © 1965 Dover Publications, Inc.

practice that allowed the architect to leave most matters of construction to the builders. The other was the consensus that appropriate building form was grounded in antiquity, itself largely the result of the arguments of Humanists like Alberti. The Renaissance architect had therefore neither to concern himself much with construction techniques, nor defend his basic design principles.

Although architecture and building have changed rather a lot since Alberti's time, the principle (if not the practice) of separating design from construction has largely remained intact and with it the need for drawing to convey the designers' ideas to builders. The Albertian conception of the architect as form-giver persists, but as building has become more complex, architects have been obliged to take a greater interest in construction technique in order to realize their formal ideas. The accepted authority of antiquity faded in the 17th Century and now the question of the sources of form became one of architecture's central problematics. Contemporary architects therefore have two tasks in addition to that set for them by Alberti: to specify construction techniques and to persuade others of the validity of the forms they propose. Their drawings thus have two functions, didactic and polemical, that have new importance in the context of construction.

In appearance, the graphics of basic construction drawings have changed little since the Renaissance. Two-dimensional representations are still the rule. Orthographic projection has been placed on a consistent mathematical footing, but the practical effect of this on the majority of construction drawings is nil. Although architects now have both the descriptive and constructive means of building more complex forms, prismatic volumes still constitute the vast bulk of the built environment (Figure 2.36). This is in large measure due to the ease of describing these forms by means of orthographic projection. On the other hand, the need to illustrate construction has changed construction drawings a great deal, adding types of drawings not used before. The building section, used until relatively recently chiefly as a means of showing an interior elevation (Figure 2.37), has become a key type of drawing because it shows the interior of walls. Poché, the graphical device by which architects told builders essentially "you know what goes here" has been replaced by a graphic language that *shows* the builders "what goes here." This graphic language has been enhanced by written notes and dimensions. The linguistic aspect of drawing has become paramount. Construction drawings

FIGURE 2.36 The prismatic massing of most contemporary buildings is evident in this aerial photograph of Manhattan.

Source: Photo by Eric Drost.

have become legal documents whose interpretation is strictly governed by convention and precedent, in which ambiguity is to be avoided.

Today it has become rare to find any expressive intention in construction drawings, but there are exceptions. Like any language, this kind of drawing has not only a semantics (the meaning of its symbols) and a syntax (rules for their assembly into larger meaningful units) but also a poetics that addresses the expressive potential of choices permitted by the first two. In the working drawings of Glenn Murcutt, for example, the careful composition of the dimensions and notes echoes the outlines of the drawing. The drawing contains an enormous amount of information while presenting the building's form as its dominant image. The final effect conveys intense study devoted to the realization of the form (echoed by the care given to the creation of the drawing) and the desire to communicate clearly and concisely (Figure 2.38).

The polemical function of drawing is especially important during the early stages of a project when architects are formulating their approach

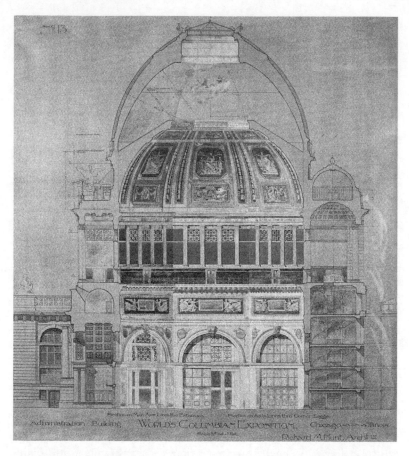

FIGURE 2.37 R. M. Hunt, section of Administration Building, World Columbian Exhibition. Late 19th-Century Beaux-Arts-trained architects like Hunt relied on masons and carpenters to construct their buildings, showing only poché where the structure would be. Building sections therefore served chiefly to show interior elevations.

Source: © American Institute of Architects Foundation.

to a design. They are still engaged in the process of moving back and forth between idea and sketch; the ideas are not yet clear. They need to present ideas to their clients and collaborators while reserving a space to continue their exploration. The purpose of polemical drawings in this context is to express ideas on this level, to make them tangible as well as visible, to allow their discussion and persuade others to accept them. They represent

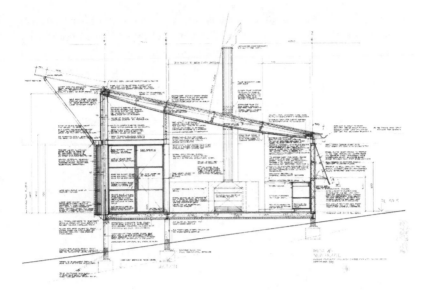

FIGURE 2.38 Glenn Murcutt, Simpson-Lee House, cross-section (1989–94). Unlike Hunt (Figure 2.37), a contemporary architect like Murcutt must show construction details and finds expressive possibilities in them. The types of information the drawing must contain are beautifully coordinated to augment the basic drawing without obscuring it in any way.

Source: Glenn Murcutt, Courtesy Architecture Foundation Australia.

the emergence of architectural ideas from the private world of the architect into the public world in which the building will exist (Figures 2.39, 2.40, 2.41).

Somehow, the architect's ideas and intentions must survive the tortuous journey from the rich ambiguity of personal exploration, through convention-bound communication and finally to the rigid requirements of contract documents. The continued centrality of drawings has given the architect the means to do this by granting him control over the flow of information. Initially, polemical drawings help build the architect's relationship with the client and other constituents, whose trust is essential if the architect is to have any control over the design. Throughout the project, the architect decides what information to share with whom and when. He becomes the gatekeeper of information generation and distribution, most of which takes place through drawings: developing the

design, sharing information, coordinating consultants' work, and inform-
ing the client of the project's progress. The architect has the opportunity
to review every such transfer of information before it takes place and
determine its content and timing. In this central position, the architect is
also the only person who has a comprehensive view of the project at any
time, lending their judgments unique weight. When the drawings are
issued for bid, the architect has determined what information they contain.
The experienced architect knows how to select and exclude information

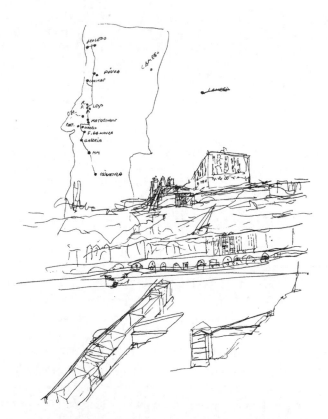

FIGURE 2.39 Alvaro Siza, sketch of Porto (1988). This drawing describes the
project's site at various scales: within the country, within the city and in its
immediate context. The architect establishes the project's roots in its site at
every scale.

Source: Image © Alvaro Siza.

FIGURE 2.40 Le Corbusier, letter to Mme. Meyer (with illustrations) of proposed villa (later Villa Meyer). Le Corbusier explains his ideas to his client in words and sketches, choosing the medium that best expresses each idea.

Source: © 2013 Artists Rights Society (ARS), New York/ADAGP, Paris/F.L.C.

FIGURE 2.41 Steve Holl, concept sketch for Knut Hamsun Center (1994). In addition to the other reasons for choosing watercolor (see Figure 2.25), this sketch also conveys a sense of openness, of investigation, inviting discussion and the participation of the client.

Source: © Steven Holl.

so as to preserve the design intent while observing the legal strictures that relate the drawings to the work of the contractor. At every stage of a project, drawing gives the architect control of the flow of information and thus the ability to see to the integrity of the design intent throughout the process.

Despite the enormous changes in building production over the past 500 years, this system maintains architects in a position of creative authorship that is, in principle, similar to that of their predecessors. The similarity, however, masks profound shifts in architects' pragmatic role in this production. Many architects cling to some version of the old image of the architect as a thinker who knows *why* a given form is appropriate or correct, but the criteria for this *why* have changed categorically. Technical matters, in which the architect is usually not the expert, exert great influence on form, allowing other designers to impinge upon the architect's authority. Esthetics is now considered a subject of speculation rather than knowledge. Still, there is a felt need for buildings to be somehow significant and society looks to architects to provide this even as it diminishes their ability to do so. However, architects also owe their central position to pragmatic concerns that arise from the evolving nature of building production. The increasingly collaborative nature of building production creates the need for a leader whose chief responsibility is to coordinate the work of ever-expanding project teams and this administrative role has devolved upon architects. The position of architects also has a legal basis that answers the business needs of owners. Architects' authority over builders derives largely from the fact that their drawings are part of a contract that builders must fulfill. Their authority over other designers is established by the latter's customary status as consultants hired by the architect. Not the least important result of this arrangement (at least in the US) is the establishment of architects' legal responsibility for the adequacy of their designs, giving owners recourse for alleged design failures. The bases for architects' centrality to building production are now largely a function of the structural requirements of our system of building production, rather than a belief in their knowledge of the principles of form.

The growing complexity of both building technology and the nature of building problems have gradually overwhelmed the drawing-based building production system. Many attempts have been made to modify the system to improve its ability to meet these challenges. In the 1980s, CAD made drawing production faster, so document sets could contain more drawings and address construction in greater detail. This came at the expense of the craft of drawing and all that it meant to architecture. New methods of project delivery have been put into practice that attempt to overcome the inefficiencies of a strict separation between design and construction. These inevitably tend to displace architects from the central position that allowed them to endow projects with coherent design intent. The fact that their position has become a function of the structural needs of the building production system rather than a perceived innate value of their knowledge has made architects' position subject to changes in those needs. Now the building production system is changing due to the introduction of new technologies—building information modeling and computational design—and therefore architects are finding that their role is changing as well.

Conclusion

This overview of some of the intimate connections between drawing and architecture should not be taken as nostalgia or Luddism. The digital tools that are changing building production open fascinating new terrain for architecture. In any event, their use is rapidly becoming standard practice in the profession. Individual architects will always be free to forego or limit their use. Drawing can be, and often is, integrated with digital design processes. The question is whether drawing, and representation in general, will remain integral to architectural work, or be supplanted by digital tools. Digital tools engage our minds and bodies very differently than drawing. Their adoption in place of drawing will change our very conception of architecture. Changing the means by which ideas are translated into form will transform the very nature of an architectural idea. Transferring geometry from the mind to the computer will profoundly alter the connection among mind, eye, and hand that drawing creates. The bodily experience of drawing that grants architects access to the haptic aspects of architecture and the world of physical making may be lost. Lastly, the professional identity and activity of the architect will be profoundly altered.

One can view these prospects in two ways. From the perspective of someone who understands architecture through drawing, these are challenges to be met by new practices and technologies that endow digital design with the key properties of drawing, either by retaining drawing itself in some way, or by inventing digital tools that provide similar experiences. To someone more interested in the possibilities of digital tools, this is an opportunity to embrace simulation and its consequences and see where they lead. It is likely that both avenues will be explored to the enrichment of architecture.

Notes

1 Wittgenstein (1922, no. 4.1212).
2 Frascari (2007, p. 3).
3 Bovelet (2010, p. 78).
4 Evans (1995, p. 165).
5 In Western music, the separation of two pitches is always a multiple of the half-step. There is no note, for example, between F and F#. Likewise, any duration must be some multiple or simple fraction of the beat.

6 Bovelet (2010, p. 75).

7 Bovelet (2010).

8 "By drawing, traces are laid for a discourse by making a design idea visible and thus publicly debatable. The public discourse is the only scale against which a design can be judged" (Bovelet, 2010, p. 80).

9 According to Michel de Certeau:

> [F]or the last four centuries all scientific enterprise has included among its traits the production of autonomous linguistic artifacts (its own specific languages and discourses) with an ability to transform the things and bodies from which they had been distinguished.
>
> (quoted in Fitzsimons, 2010, p. 14)

10 "We need not construe architecture as a purely scientific undertaking to recognize that architectural drawing functions like one of these 'linguistic artifacts' . . . specifically, architectural drawing has linguistic properties insofar as its conventions allow us to share ideas" (Fitzsimons, 2010, p. 14).

11 Evans (1995, p. 1210).

12 "[P]rojection was a late, extra ingredient grasping more or less cautiously at the imaginary space behind the three drawings [of plan, elevation and section]" (Evans, 1995, p. 118).

13 Evans (1995, p. 38).

14 Kant (1929, 198 (A163/B203)).

15 Evans, *The Projective Cast: Architecture and Its Three Geometries* (1995).

16 "Primary forms are beautiful forms because they can be clearly appreciated" (Le Corbusier, 1986, p. 23).

17 (Husserl, 1970, p. 26).

18 Plato (1965, p. 71), *Timaeus* 20.

19 C. Wright Mills, quoted in Sennett (2008, p. 27).

20 Sennett (2008, p. 38).

21 Sennett (2008, p. 110.

22 Merleau-Ponty (1962, p. 98 ff.).

23 Henri Matisse, quoted in Pallasmaa (2009, p. 92).

24 Levin (1993).

25 Pallasmaa (2009, p. 15).

26 Juhani Pallasmaa puts it thus:

> Touch is the unconsciousness of vision, and this hidden tactile experience determines the sensuous qualities of the perceived object. This is the hidden element in touching and the activation of tactile judgment and memory that is involved in drawing.
>
> (2009, p. 102)

27 Sennett (2008, pp. 194–195).

28 "Doodles" are expressions of the compulsion to draw and an implicit acknowledgement of drawing's power. By terming a drawing a doodle, the drawer evinces a need to renounce that power.

29 Frascari (2007, p. 4).

30 Alberti (1966).

3

BUILDING INFORMATION MODELING

In 2004, a study by the National Institute of Standards and Technology found that failures in information communication had cost building owners in the US $15.8 billion in a single year.[1] This report simply put a number on the cost of a trend that owners had been aware of for years. A White Paper issued by a major association of building owners later in the same year made an issue of this trend and called for the use of computer technology to overcome it.[2] This report envisaged not only improving the quality of construction documents, but linking the entire building life-cycle from design through operation by a continuous flow of digital information. Although comparatively undeveloped at the time, building information modeling (BIM) technology was seized upon as a solution to these problems. BIM was seen as a step towards solving such problems because they are essentially problems of information management, which is BIM's forte.

BIM is a computer technology that simulates a building's perfor-mance. Here, performance refers to any measure of a building's response to any aspect of its environment broadly understood, embracing condi-tions of climate, physical demands, program, budget, legal requirements, human interactions and institutions within the AECOO industry.[3] Performance can be viewed from the perspective of any of the project's participants, starting with that of the owner who initiates it, through those of its designers and builders, down to that of its end users and the public that is indirectly affected by it. By simulating performance, BIM tends to focus the effort of the entire project development process on establishing and meeting performance criteria. Some aspects of building lend themselves naturally to the notion of performance, particularly technical and financial considerations which are quantitative and can have clear criteria set for them. Other aspects of building are far less amenable to this kind of evaluation: the qualitative, subjective, and expressive dimensions of design that form the heart of traditional architectural values. Recasting the building design problem as a matter of performance profoundly shifts the values underlying design. This recasting was well under way before the advent of BIM.

The Limitations of Drawing and the Origins of BIM

Architectural drawing had its origins in Renaissance assumptions about architectural form and building practice. Architects of that time understood their role as prescribing form and they relied on builders' traditional knowledge to work out the physical construction. All that architects needed to provide were the dimensions and disposition of traditionally constructed elements along with details of ornamentation (Figure 3.1). Consequently, architectural drawing was developed to describe form, and only certain kinds of form at that.[4]

As buildings became more complex technical objects, they required more information of a non-formal nature for their construction. The increasing complexity of certain types of buildings in the latter half of the 19th Century began to strain the ability of drawings to document all the information needed for construction. This trend accelerated rapidly and became acute in the second half of the 20th Century. An array of specialists was eventually needed to design all of the component systems of a building. Construction expertise likewise became distributed among a large number of specialized subcontractors. Builders came to rely on the design documents for far more information than form. Construction document sets came to require many more drawings and these required extensive augmentation in the form of text (notes and specifications) to convey all this new information. The responsibility devolved upon architects for eliminating omissions and conflicts among (in some cases) hundreds of sheets of drawings and thousands of pages of specifications,

FIGURE 3.1 Andrea Palladio, Plate XV, Book 4 of the *Four Books of Architecture* (Temple of Nerva Trajanus).

Source: © 1965 Dover Publications, Inc.

produced by dozens of individual designers and draftsmen working in several different firms. This eventually became a superhuman task for projects of any size or complexity. Construction documents across the industry gradually declined in quality, causing more change orders and delays and increasing costs for owners.

Owners were concerned not only about the direct costs of change orders and delays due to poor construction documents, but also the uncertainty these created about a building's final cost and delivery date. There was also uncertainty as to whether the building would meet all the owner's needs as set forth in the building's space program. Finally, owners wanted to know with greater accuracy how much it would cost to operate their buildings over their lifespan (about 70–75% of the cost of constructing and owning a building lies in its operation and maintenance). All of these uncertainties made planning a project difficult and therefore riskier financially. The recognition of the scope of the problem caused large building owners to demand improvements in construction documents as well as better predictions of buildings' total cost of ownership.

Software that is loosely and somewhat inaccurately called "BIM" is now becoming commonplace in architectural practices and architecture schools throughout the world. As of this writing, BIM is rapidly gaining acceptance in the building industries of industrialized countries including the US. In 2009, 48% of U.S. architecture firms and about half of construction companies reported using BIM in some fashion, and these numbers are growing rapidly.[5] The extent of BIM use varies widely from firm to firm and project to project. Larger and more complex projects tend to make more advanced use of BIM. In 2010, it was reported that 83% of the 300 largest AE firms in the US were using BIM.[6] Although many architects and architecture students use this software daily, many do not fully grasp its nature and how it affects the role of architects in the building production process. It may therefore be useful to develop a description of BIM from the ground up in order to clarify its functional basis and emerging role in the contemporary building industry.

The Organization of BIM

The key to understanding BIM is that its fundamental purpose is to facilitate business processes in the building industry by organizing information flows throughout the building lifecycle. It is this purpose that drives the design and use of BIM software, not its role as an architect's design tool *per se*. BIM may be defined as "a modeling technology and associated set of processes to produce, communicate and analyze *building models*." [7] A building model in this context is a digital database that contains building information. This information is in *computable* form, meaning that it can be processed (not just stored) by computers.[8] To meet the challenge of creating a continuous flow of data throughout the building cycle, building information needs to be shared among many different groups, each with their own particular needs: architects, engineers, owners, cost estimators, contractors, fabricators, manufacturers, building officials, leasing agents, facilities managers, and others. Creating a single model that contains all of this information is awkward due to its size, but is fortunately unnecessary. Each of these groups can instead create its own model and share parts of it with the others in a so-called *federated model* (Figure 3.2). Each group contributes its share to the federated model so that the entire team can see each group's information. Given their different needs, it is likely that each group will use different software applications. These will therefore need to be able to exchange data with other BIM-related applications. This capability, called *interoperability*, turns out to be crucial to the overall project of BIM. It can also be difficult to implement.

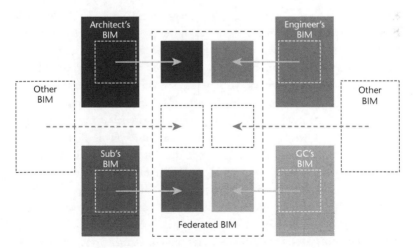

FIGURE 3.2 Diagram of a federated BIM model.

Source: © Author.

A building model is composed of *objects*. Each object usually represents a single building component such as a wall or a door. In this context, an "object" is a piece of computer code that carries "geometric definitions and associated data and rules." [9] The geometric definitions determine the object's shape. The rules provide the object with "intelligence" that govern relationships among the object's parts, the object's interaction with other objects and how the object is displayed in various contexts. Much of the data an object carries are assigned values by the user. Such data are called *parameters* and objects containing these are called *parametric*. Object intelligence may also constrain the values of certain parameters so that they conform to real-world conditions. A door object, for example, may only permit standard values for its width. To give a concrete example of how this works: a door object's parameters include its leaf and frame dimensions, construction, materials, cost, and so forth (Figure 3.3). Its intelligence causes it to relate the dimensions of the door and frame, align one edge of the leaf with one edge of the frame, allow the leaf to rotate around this edge, and so on. Intelligence also allows the door to create an opening in the wall where it is placed. The object's geometric definition uses some of the rules and parameters to generate the outlines of the door in space. Because building models are composed of parametric objects, the models themselves are called parametric models.

A BIM *platform* (or *authoring tool*) is a piece of software that creates building models and displays them in a variety of formats. These include visualizations, drawings, tables and schedules, and digital data. Each display of a model or a portion of it, regardless of its format, is called a *model view*. All model views are generated by the BIM platform from the information contained in a set of objects in the model. Because the software displays information contained in a set of objects, any model view of those objects will be consistent with any other. This feature alone alleviates one problem that dogs large drawing sets: the difficulty of coordinating many different drawings of the same piece of construction. Architects usually work with a particular class of BIM platforms (unsurprisingly called architectural BIM authoring tools). This is to distinguish them from authoring tools used by other disciplines and the universe of other BIM tools used for purposes other than design and documentation.

The fact that building models are based on parametric objects has several important consequences. First, a single object can create an

Geometric description

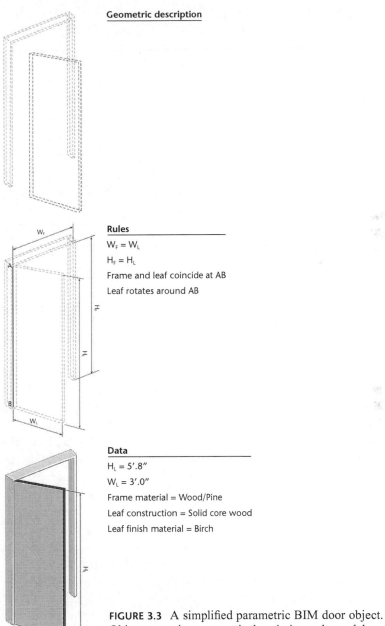

Rules

$W_F = W_L$

$H_F = H_L$

Frame and leaf coincide at AB

Leaf rotates around AB

Data

$H_L = 5'.8''$

$W_L = 3'.0''$

Frame material = Wood/Pine

Leaf construction = Solid core wood

Leaf finish material = Birch

FIGURE 3.3 A simplified parametric BIM door object.
Objects contain a geometric description, rules and data.

Source: © Author.

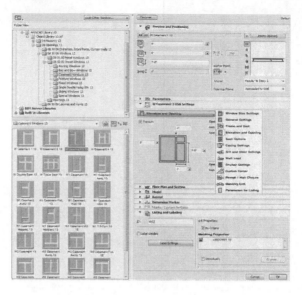

FIGURE 3.4 This window describes a parametric BIM window object. By choosing different values for its various parameters, this single object can generate an enormous range of windows.

Source: © Author.

infinite number of building components. By varying its parameters, one window object can generate windows of different dimensions and materials (Figure 3.4). The BIM platform, therefore, does not need to contain a very large number of basic objects in order for the architect to create a wide range of building components. Second, parameters can be used in calculations to find other information of interest. For example, the dimensions of a space can be used to calculate its volume. Material quantity take-offs can be done by summing up the amount of a particular material (found from each object's material and dimensional parameters) throughout the model. Parameters can also be generated from other parameters. A modern Alberti, for example, might implement a system of proportions by using one parameter (the length of one side of a room, the height of a column) to generate another that bears a proportional relationship to it (the second side of the room, the diameter of the column). Third, object intelligence can help the designer avoid both tedious work and potential errors. Once a stair is inserted in a model, for example, the designer does not have to draw any of its representations. The object's code generates these representations intelligently depending on the model view in question. Unlike in drawing, where, say, a plan view and section view of a stair are drawn separately and therefore may contain conflicting information, in BIM, these two views are generated automatically from the same object and therefore cannot conflict with each other. Tedious, error-prone tasks such as counting the number of doors of a given type in a building can be done by automatically searching for doors with identical parameters.

BIM confers these advantages when used by itself within an architect's office. Useful as they are, they are only the beginning. To achieve the goal of creating a flow of data throughout the building's lifecycle, many different groups of people must be able to handle and modify building data. BIM data must move from one group to another, preserving relevant information. This has proven to be the single greatest obstacle to the implementation of BIM.

Babel to BIM: Interoperability

Each participant in a design and construction process is interested in different types of data. Even a single building component such as a light fixture has different types of information associated with it that are of interest to different members of a project team: the architect needs its form and location; the lighting designer, its output; the owner, its power consumption; the electrical engineer, its power requirements; the electrician, its manufacturer and cost; the building maintenance manager, the type of lamp and its life expectancy. Each individual along the chain can provide some of this information and no one needs all of it. There is a hand-off at various stages of the building lifecycle at which the current information is winnowed to fit the needs of the person receiving it, who may add to it to suit that person's needs. Nor is this process linear. The process of designing the lighting, locating the fixtures, specifying them, and providing them with power requires the simultaneous input of the architect, lighting designer, and electrical engineer. In short, the flow of information is complex with different requirements by different participants at various stages of the project. The problem is to allow information to flow through this process so that everyone gets what they need from those upstream in a form they can use, and passes it on in a form that can be used by those downstream.

The main obstacle to achieving this information utopia is the diversity of forms the information takes. In the past, everything was on paper and using it required a human to interpret drawings or text—a time-consuming and error-prone process. With the advent of computers, much of it was digitized, but in different formats chosen according to the needs of each specialized group without regard for others. Information was therefore transferred on paper or in digital format that had to be read by a human. To automate this process, a common digital format is needed that can be understood by the software being used by anyone in the chain. Given the specialized origin of the software in use and cultural resistance to change, this is a gigantic challenge. Interoperability is needed for BIM to fulfill its promise of streamlining the flow of information throughout the building lifecycle.

Achieving interoperability is a complex task. It is always difficult to change how people do business, in this case, both in the building industry and among software developers. There is a chicken-and-egg problem in both finding the resources to develop interoperable standards and the advantages of continuing to do business as usual. Most everyone agrees that interoperability is a worthy goal, but most everyone also sees a near-term advantage in sticking to tried-and-true methods.

There are two current approaches to achieving interoperability: file-based exchanges and federated models, also called model repositories.[10] These two methods respond to different requirements. File-based exchanges are designed to transfer detailed model data from one platform to another, preserving as much object intelligence as possible. They are used to share data about details of design or construction. Model repositories contain project-level information allowing coordination of major building systems to avoid clashes among them and scheduling and tracking progress of their construction. They consolidate data from the individual BIMs created by members of the project team, preserving each object's geometry but show little object intelligence other than the system to which it belongs and its identification. They allow information to be added to objects, typically that which concerns their construction, installation, or operation.

File-based exchanges allow BIM platforms to exchange files by means of an intermediate, mutually intelligible file format. To work for the entire industry, this format must be an *open standard*—one that is freely available to everyone. There are a few standard formats now available for such exchanges. The most widely used are IFC (Industry Foundation Classes) and CIS/2, a format developed specifically for data exchanges within the steel industry. IFC is a general standard that can, in principle, handle any kind of building data. There are several challenges to the implementation of IFC. In order to be as flexible as possible, IFC allows multiple ways of describing a piece of construction. Therefore rules for specific exchanges (for example, from architect to structural engineer) are needed, called model view definitions or MVDs. An MVD tells a BIM platform how to describe a piece of construction for export to an IFC file and passes this information to the receiving platform to allow its importation. For some exchanges, an MVD can be created on the fly by a platform's IFC export and import engines. Other exchanges require a customized MVD, which require specialized expertise to create. Given the number and specificity of exchanges that might be needed for a project, IFC exchange can be a complicated process that many architects do not understand. The alternative is to use a proprietary file format that can be used by both platforms, meaning that the same software developer has created both platforms or has licensed its format to a third party. In this case architects and others must rely on this software developer to anticipate their needs.

Some European countries (Norway and Finland, for example) have established effective IFC standards for their building industries. In the US, public support for standards development has been lacking, and the implementation of BIM is currently hampered by a lack of interoperability that limits the technology's utility and has caused its uneven adoption. Design and construction teams are steadily overcoming these problems using a variety of approaches including single-vendor solutions, IFC exchanges, XML schemas, model repositories, spreadsheets, customized APIs and web services. In order to fulfill BIM's purpose of facilitating information flows through the building lifecycle, what is needed is real-time collaboration using online data accessible whenever and wherever a project participant needs it.

The final step in the information chain is transferring information from the construction BIM to the owner for use in facilities management (operating and maintaining the building). This step, like the others, is hindered by the variety of methods owners use to manage their facilities. These range from the totally manual to sophisticated computerized maintenance management systems (CMMS). This is being addressed by an IFC MVD created for this purpose called the Construction Owners Building Information Exchange (COBie).[11]

The American Institute of Steel Construction (AISC) took the unusual step of commissioning the creation of a file exchange format specifically designed to unify the structural steel production chain: structural design and specification, detailing, fabrication, milling, delivery, and erection. This format, called CIS/2, even permits fabricators to substitute digital models for shop drawings, facilitating and in some cases automating the tedious process of shop drawing review for engineers. Since the checked model is used for fabrication, there can be no discrepancies.

Architecture as Information

In a sense, information has always been at the center of architecture. The Albertian system of drawing could be viewed as a means of transmitting information from architects to builders. It was not seen in these terms at the time, however, due to the fact that a building was considered to be an identical copy of the design.[12] Builders were tools in the hands of the architect, as it were, a kind of pantographic mechanism that transferred the design precisely from drawing to material. The building could therefore be considered the creation of the architect. Even though few if any buildings were actually built in strict accordance with this schema, it was the basis of the architect's claim to authorship of a building that was accepted for centuries. Now, however, the vast amount of information associated with building has led to a gradual recognition of the collaborative nature of its creation, with the consequent transformation of the idea of the architect as author into something resembling that of the composer–conductor leading an orchestra, whose artistic achievement consists not only in conceiving the desired result but also in eliciting a great performance from a group of specialized, creative individuals.

Understanding building as an exercise in information management tends to shift its focus from the outcome to the process. It assumes the existence of an idea guiding the process that will make its outcome meaningful without providing a place in the process for the generation of such ideas. While building information management dictates the types of information that must be accommodated, the actual content of this information is irrelevant to its management. This appears to leave design itself wide open, but this is reckoning without the performative basis of

BIM. Casting all building information in the form of computable data serves performativity in two ways. First, it enables the quantitative evaluation of the performance of various aspects of a design. Second, it eliminates inefficiencies in the movement of information with a project by making this movement automatic. In doing the latter, BIM leads to a fundamentally different configuration of the building professions than prevailed under the domain of drawing.

As pointed out in Chapter 2, the architect's traditional position as the author of a building (and hence the leader of a project) had not only a theoretical basis, but also a pragmatic one as the central information manager. The architect controlled who had what information, when they received it, and in what form. Only the architect had a comprehensive view of the entire project, giving his design judgment unique authority. This became increasingly important as buildings became more complex and eventually eclipsed Albertian principles as the grounds for his authority.

The initial or conceptual design process was particularly important in establishing the architect's position in the project. Typically, the owner hired an architect or architecture firm that developed the initial (or conceptual) design according to the owner's needs. Once this was done, consultants were brought in as needed to design various technical building systems. The owner and the architect thus established a working relationship before any other parties to the design process were involved. Contractors, if they participated at this point at all, were also used as consultants to provide cost and constructability advice. More typically, a professional cost estimator was engaged by the architect to provide this input, preserving a strict separation between design and construction. This arrangement gave the architect considerable authority in the owner's eyes.

The five traditional standard project phases of the architect's work—schematic design, design development, construction documents, bidding/negotiation, and contract administration—are predicated on drawing-based information flow. They presume a particular starting point and a definite order in which information is added to the project, proceeding from the general to the specific. The project develops at a consistent rate across all of its aspects to avoid making assumptions that will be overturned later in the process. Architects and other designers typically know a great deal more than they show in conceptual and schematic level drawings. They omit this information in early phase drawings because the considerable time invested in drawing it will be lost if the design's configuration changes, as is likely in its early stages. The drawing process does not provide a means of storing this "excess" information in the drawings. Such information must be stored separately and retrieved or recreated later, causing a kind of information loss in transitions from one phase to another (Figure 3.5). The most acute is in the transition from design to construction, due to contractual constraints that result from using drawings to convey design information.

By allowing information to be stored continuously throughout the project's development, BIM eliminates the information loss inherent in a drawing-based process. There is now no reason to withhold information until a later stage: the BIM can store and retrieve it as needed. It also greatly facilitates making changes. If a schematic level drawing is wanted, a model view containing only the appropriate information can be created. The traditional five phases are no longer relevant. BIM-based projects do not move from general to specific information across the board. There

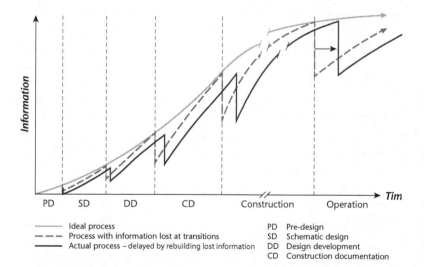

FIGURE 3.5 This diagram schematically illustrates the loss of information that takes place at the transition between phases in a traditional design and construction process. The curve represents the ideal process in which information is steadily accumulated with no loss throughout the project.

Source: © Author.

may be very specific information in certain areas and little or no information in others. The five-phase model has been enshrined in contracts and industry custom and is difficult to replace, though the attempt to do so is in progress.[13]

Information stored in the model early leads to one of the great advantages of BIM from the owner's point of view: this information can be analyzed to allow more accurate understanding of several important project parameters much earlier in the process than drawing would allow. This, coupled with the speed with which such analyses can be carried out by computers, makes it possible to compare a number of conceptual design alternatives according to criteria such as program compliance, building orientation, energy consumption, sustainability, cost, and time to construct. In itself, making design decisions earlier reduces cost, since the earlier decisions are made, the less they cost to implement (Figure 3.6). Such early evaluations give the owner greater certainty about the project's performance, cost and suitability to its purpose, all of which contribute to its overall economy.

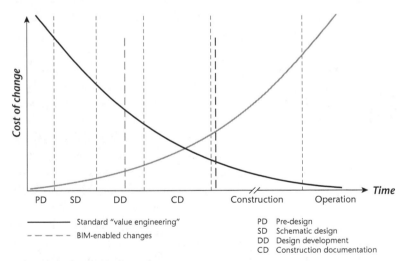

FIGURE 3.6 Changes cost more and have smaller scope as a project is developed. In a traditional process, changes are made later due to insufficient information to make them earlier. BIM provides that information earlier in the process, allowing changes to be made when they are less expensive and more effective.

Source: © Author.

One can imagine a future in which the entire design-construction process will be accomplished solely with digital information, but that future is a long way off for many reasons. Some of these are technical, which will likely be resolved in due course. Others are cultural, rooted in customary practices that people are reluctant to abandon. Some of these are enshrined in law. Others are economic, deriving from the reliance (in the US at least) on market forces to drive innovation. Investing in the development of open standards is a losing proposition for a private company or corporation. It will incur all the costs while everyone will enjoy the benefits. Open standards is a type of infrastructure that would benefit the entire construction industry. Similar infrastructure has been created in the past by public investment (interstate highways, the internet). Such an investment would seem to be warranted in this case.

In the meantime, drawings are and will be essential to the construction process for some time to come, and current BIM platforms are designed to generate drawings. "Drawings" generated from BIMs are model views equivalent to any other model view, not freestanding drawings in the traditional sense. Computers can easily generate geometric projections, but traditional plans, sections and elevations are not merely projections. They rely on certain conventions which, as it turns out, are very difficult for software designers to accommodate. A simple thing, such as using line weights to create a sense of depth in a drawing, can only be achieved in BIM by awkward patches or linework added manually to a generated projection. Another such problem occurs in plans where conventions dictate what elements above or below the level at which the plan is taken are shown and how. These problems can be traced back to the fact that, whereas construction drawing is a language devised for human communication (with the conventional basis this implies), BIM is based on the need to make all information computable, i.e. capable of being processed by computers. BIM software mimics drawing to accommodate architects and others accustomed to drawing; it is not its native language. From the perspective of BIM technology, creating drawings is an unnecessary detour, a concession to humans who, as it were, speak an archaic language. There are many other model views, more congenial to the software's operation, that can provide designers with views of a project: purely geometric projections, renderings, 3D prints, and numerical analyses. BIM's power lies in its ability to perform calculations on building data of all kinds. Its *telos* is the automation of the entire building industry. Like all technologies, its *raison d'être* is efficiency, something the construction industry has conspicuously lacked in the past. And, like all technologies, it is up to architects and others in the building industry to decide what uses will be made of it.

Collaboration

Design and construction have always been collaborative activities. The increasing complexity of building projects has brought collaboration to the fore, requiring more specialized knowledge, and surpassing the ability of any one person to master it all. Drawing limited collaboration, in part by making the entire project dependent on the central figure of the architect to control the flow of information to the various parties to the project. While this afforded the architect control over the design, it created lags and opportunities for transcription errors that made collaboration inefficient. By replacing drawings and text with computable data, BIM creates very different conditions for collaboration, in which building information can be exchanged directly and instantaneously and with no need for intermediate transcription. This requires each participant to rethink their role in the project, creating a very different environment for design and construction.

One result is a more level project team structure in which all participants contribute and use information on an equal basis. If the general contractor (and perhaps some of the major subcontractors) can participate, the design process benefits by having constantly updated cost and constructability information. Whereas with drawing the distribution of information was carefully controlled by the architect, information is now transparent and quickly available to everyone. Even in such a "flat" team structure, there is a need for a leader or coordinator. However, this need not be the architect as he has no special access to information. There are several possible project leaders: the owner's representative, the general contractor, a construction manager, or the architect. Design decisions can be made collaboratively since everyone has access to the relevant information. This implies a different relationship between design and construction, reducing the hallowed separation between them.[14]

Realizing this project structure requires fundamental changes in the way construction contracts are written. Traditional contracts were based on the assumption that the owner's financial interests were best safeguarded by competitive bidding among contractors. This prevented the bidding contractors from participating in design. Recently, project delivery methods that allow greater collaboration among designers and contractors[15] have been more widely used, recognizing that the owner's best interest often lies in certainty about the project's result, cost and schedule rather than lowest bid price. BIM invites even greater cooperation among designers, contractors, and owners to ensure that the owner gets the facility it wants with a reliable budget and schedule. This allows the owner to plan the project effectively. A new project delivery method, called Integrated Project Delivery (IPD), unites the major parties to a project to define the project's scope and design collaboratively.[16] This takes advantage of the knowledge of all participants during the planning and design phases to produce a project that meets the owner's needs in terms of program, budget, and timing.

As of this writing, full IPD is rarely fully realized in the US, although more collaborative processes are becoming common. The ideal of a fully integrated, collaborative design–construction–operation process is usually most closely approached in large, complex projects. In such projects, many tasks that were traditionally done through drawings are done digitally. These can include coordination, scheduling, shop drawings, visualization, and fabrication.

Effects on Architectural Practice

Traditionally, architecture was practiced by single individuals or in small workshops. These practices existed to implement the singular vision of one architect. Others who worked in the firm did so under the tutelage of this "master," as Frank Lloyd Wright regarded Louis Sullivan. The structure of these practices—a clear hierarchy of master, disciples, and draftsmen—suited the goal of realizing this singular vision. Of course, this goal had to be pursued in the context of the building industry as a whole. Until recently, the building industry was organized around this image of the singular architect. These master architects also generally commanded greater respect and authority from owners and builders than they do today. The reasons for the present diminished status of architects can be found in the very same processes that led to the adoption of BIM.

Around the beginning of the 20th Century, larger firms began to appear in response to the growing complexity of construction and the resulting need to provide an increasing diversity of services.[17] Individuals in these firms became more specialized. As these trends developed, a single architect's vision became increasingly inadequate as a firm's organizing principle. The staff of a large firm could not have the close relationship with a master needed for them to absorb his way of thinking. Furthermore, the notion of a sole designer became untenable as design became inherently collaborative, due to the many factors affecting a building's design. The size of the firm, in conjunction with the complexity of its projects, brought problems of organization to the fore. A set of procedures was needed to ensure that standards were met regardless of the individual who happened to occupy a particular position at a given time. Much architectural labor was thus commodified. The organization of the firm itself became a major factor in its ability (or lack thereof) to realize design ideas. Often, efficient organization became an end in itself. This dovetailed with the evolving structure of the building industry, which came to require more detailed and technical information from architects, a task for which large, diverse and well-organized firms were best suited to provide. The growing market and an increasingly industrialized industry demanded a large number of more or less interchangeable firms capable of providing these services.

The changes BIM is bringing to the organization of the building industry are of a magnitude not seen before in modern history. The organization of an architectural practice oriented towards the production of information is different from that of one that produces drawings.[18] The traditional drawing-based process involves clear phases and transitions between them. BIM-based projects develop continuously with no definite internal benchmarks.[19] The defined phases of drawing-based projects suggested a distinction between "designers" and "production staff," with a hand-off taking place at the transition from design development to construction documentation. Many firms rejected this division of labor; however, even in firms where there is no such formal division, *de facto* specializations tend to develop. By contrast, BIM places a great premium on all design team members having a comprehensive understanding of the project. The disappearance of distinct phases demands that architects understand the project at many levels throughout its development. As the initial model evolves into the final construction model, each addition to it ideally anticipates its future elaboration, its use in various analyses, and its export for sharing with other team members. To take full advantage of

BIM, in other words, architects need to understand the construction of both the building and of the model and apply that understanding consistently throughout the project. The knowledge base and skill set of architects using BIM are therefore different than those needed for drawing.

Organizing a practice to make effective use of BIM requires a thorough rethinking of workflows, project staffing and scheduling, contracts with clients and consultants, procurement of software and hardware, staff training, billing, and marketing. For example, more work is done in the earlier stages of a project using BIM compared with drawing (Figure 3.7), so that a greater proportion of the firm's project-related expenses are incurred earlier. BIM can also provide a wealth of information for firm management. It can provide means of tracking the progress of a project very closely. By mining the data stored in its BIMs over a period of time, the firm can identify factors that influence construction cost, internal cost and profitability, schedule, and others.

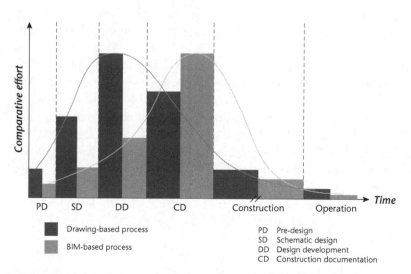

FIGURE 3.7 To gather the information that allows designers and owners to make early decisions in a BIM-based process, the designers must do more work early in the process. The portion of the total work done before construction documents increases and that done during construction documents decreases with BIM.

Source: © Author.

Managing a BIM project is very different than managing a drawing-based one. The project manager must not only understand the construction process, but also be an expert in the use and capabilities of an architectural BIM platform as well as information exchanges using a variety of methods. Before work on a project can begin, its BIM must be designed to meet the needs of the firm's role in the project and scope of work. This design must correspond to the information the BIM will ultimately contain and the uses that will be made of it. Because these requirements vary from project to project, the architectural BIM for each project needs to be designed specifically for that project's needs. Owners often have their own requirements for the organization of information that affect the BIM's design. This need for project-specificity has to be balanced by the firm's need for consistency in its projects, both for quality assurance and for later information retrieval. Most firms develop templates for different project types that are adapted for specific projects.

Distributing work among the members of a BIM project team is not as simple as assigning drawing files to various people. Within the architectural office, team members are usually working on a single BIM. To avoid creating conflicts, each team member is assigned a portion of the model that no one else can modify. BIM platforms provide this capability, but making such assignments so as to maximize each person's efficiency is part of the art of managing a BIM process. This process is often facilitated by a *BIM server*. This is software running on a dedicated server or a workstation computer that hosts the model, controls access to it by users to avoid conflicts, and ensures its overall consistency.[20]

The intensely collaborative nature of a BIM-based project team places special demands on its members. On the technical side, they need to learn to make routine use of communication technologies and understand the mechanics of BIM information exchanges. On the human side, they have to keep in view their role in the larger project team and make collaboration a habit. This self-image of the architect as collaborator is a radical departure from the traditional idea of the architect as heroic creator. Somehow, in spite of their experience to the contrary, architects have preserved the latter idea to an absurd degree. Certainly there are creative moments in design, but the vast bulk of the work is done together with others to realize the project. One of the greatest challenges BIM presents to architects is maintaining their creative role while adapting to the collaborative nature of their work.

Many of these changes in architects' work environment and knowledge requirements concern their relationship with computer technology. Most firms today work with BIM software as designed by its developer and are satisfied to understand the technology sufficiently to implement it to meet their immediate needs. Without the ability to customize and even modify the software, these needs are determined in large part by the most apparent capabilities of the software. These architects are limited to some extent by a tool they cannot fully control. The question arises as to how well an architect needs to understand the technology. Can he treat it as a "black box" and learn to use it by rote? Does he need to understand something of its design and operation in order to make good use of it? Might he need to be able to write computer scripts or even become a skilled programmer? Some firms try to regain control by employing programmers who adapt BIM software to their specific needs and create new workflows, connecting several pieces of software to allow them to communicate with each other. Some firms have programmers (who may or may not also be architects) on their staff so that such customization is a routine part of their work. Independent consultants can also provide these services. By "getting under the hood" to make the software perform as they want it to, these firms not only free themselves from the limitations it imposes, but also open up new possibilities for architecture made possible by the technology.

BIM became an industry standard in order to solve logistical and organizational problems that were overwhelming drawing. This capability facilitates the efficient construction of almost any building and makes feasible projects that would be impossible to realize due to their complexity or sheer size. But BIM, in tandem with computational design, can expand the horizons of architectural expression as well. To achieve this, architects need to master these tools as they mastered drawing instruments so that their imaginations, rather than the tools, set the limits of what can be designed and built. Current BIM tools are limited in this respect and are bound to improve, but the limitations will never disappear entirely. No software design can possibly anticipate and accommodate all the ideas an architect may have. To truly master these tools, architects must be able to modify them to perform whatever functions they have in mind. Programming is becoming part of architecture. Approaching programming as an architectural design process is discussed further in Chapter 4.

BIM subtly but profoundly changes the nature of the services architects offer. Instead of drawings and specifications, architects' direct work product is now information in a database. This information has a much wider range of uses than simply constructing a building. During design it can be used to simulate many aspects of building performance, giving the designers and the owner greater confidence that the design is well suited to the owner's needs. It can include all of the information generated or gathered during the planning, design, and construction of a project that the owner can use to operate the building after handover.[21] Performance simulations in the model can be compared with actual building performance, allowing the owner to identify and adjust systems that are not working as designed, or to identify design flaws. In short, BIM data can add considerable value for the owner beyond the building itself. Architecture firms find themselves able to provide a wider range of services based on building lifecycle information.

BIM facilitates geographically dispersed design teams by providing electronic means of collaborating that do not depend on the location of its members. The potential market for a firm's services is now global, as is the pool of talent available to work on a project. By the same token, firms now face global competition. This globalization of design services mainly affects very large projects for which the ability to draw upon the best available expertise compensates for the additional logistical complexity and expense this involves. Interestingly, there is a growing recognition that collaboration is more effective when people are able to talk to each other as well as communicate electronically. The so-called "Big Room" where representatives of the various design team firms are located in the same place has been found to be a very productive environment.[22]

Globalization raises the question of outsourcing parts of a firm's work. With CAD, this became a widespread practice, employing CAD operators in lower-wage countries who, taking advantage of the time difference, could turn work around overnight. CAD is merely laying down two-dimensional figures. The only variables are the layer and pen to be used for each. Outsourcing BIM is quite a different story, as there are far more choices to be made by a modeler than a drafter. This is why firms must have detailed standards to ensure consistency within and across their models. An outsourcing firm must comply with each client's unique, complex BIM standards. There is the additional complication that, even within a set of standards, there are often many different ways to model a given piece of construction. These factors make it very difficult for an outsourcing firm to work on a given client's model in a manner consistent with the client's modeling practices. Even if these problems were overcome, outsourcing BIM is likely to be inefficient. As we have seen, a BIM process works best when every modeler understands the project comprehensively, both the model and the construction.

The demands of working collaboratively with co-equal partners also affect the business models of architecture firms. In this environment there is much more variation in the architect's role and scope of work from project to project.[23] This must be renegotiated for every project as each project becomes unique in its goals and organization. The actual nature and scope of an architecture firm's work on a given project are determined as much by team dynamics as by contractual terms. This changes both the terms of the firm's contract for its services and the model by which its managers determine appropriate fees. Fortunately, information gleaned by mining data from prior BIMs can help managers meet these challenges.

Another trend affecting architecture firms' business models is the blurring of the line separating design from construction. Increasingly, owners are willing to give up traditional design–bid–build project delivery in exchange for greater overall value that BIM-based processes can provide. This greater value arises in large part from the participation of the project's contractor in its design. With the constructability and cost information provided by the contractor, the owner can make informed decisions earlier when the cost of their implementation is minimal. The owner can have greater confidence in the budget and schedule developed this way since the contractor has a detailed knowledge of the project before construction begins. From the architect's point of view, the involvement of the contractor in design raises questions about who has the responsibility for the consequences of design decisions and construction methods, since more construction information will appear in the design BIM than did in a traditional set of construction documents.

The design-construction line can also be blurred from the other direction. Using BIM data, computer numerically controlled (CNC) machinery allows architects and other designers to produce building components directly. This becomes increasingly economical as designers learn to use their design data to control fabrication machinery and the latter's use in construction becomes commonplace.

Information-centric design will change the large firm–small firm dynamic. In the small firms' favor, BIM makes it possible for these firms to take on much larger projects. In favor of the large firms, their greater resources allow them to exploit the technology more effectively. They can afford the services of programmers who can customize or write new software to perform specific tasks or create customized workflows for individual projects. Large firms can also make more and better use of their data. They have the resources to maintain large databases of historical project information. These can be mined to discern patterns that can help them manage projects more effectively or assist clients in making decisions about their projects.[24] These firms can also afford to experiment with new technologies and processes that may increase their capabilities. As these firms perfect their methods, it becomes cost effective for them to take on smaller projects, taking work from smaller firms.

Conclusion

The adoption of building information modeling is rapidly changing the conditions, scope, and nature of architects' work. It is transforming their work product from building design to building information, expanding their scope beyond designing buildings to providing information to owners for the entire building lifecycle. BIM serves the needs of owners by providing hard data early in a project's development to allow them to make crucial decisions early in the process when making changes is least expensive. It also offers the possibility of using information from the design and construction process in the management of their buildings. But the architect cannot provide these benefits alone. Doing so requires intense collaboration among all the project's designers as well as the contractor. Effective collaboration entails information that is transparent and readily available to all project participants. Architects thus lose their former position as the gatekeepers of information and the sole possessors of a comprehensive view of the project. Their central position in the project is no longer assured and their role can vary from project to project.

These new conditions of practice exert specific pressures on the architect's thinking. In the data-centric, collaborative environment produced by BIM, the *lingua franca* is performance. In collective design decisions, performance criteria become the principal design goals. Aspects of the project that can be evaluated quantitatively are thereby foregrounded. They can become the chief drivers of the design if the architect does not find a way to assert other values in a way the design team can accept. There is great pressure on the architect to adopt a performative way of thinking, which leads to designing in simulation.

Notes

1　Gallaher *et al.* (2004).
2　Construction Users Roundtable (2004).
3　Architecture, Engineering, Construction, Ownership and Operations.
4　See the discussion of geometry in Chapter 2.
5　McGraw-Hill Construction (2009).
6　Building Design and Construction (2010).
7　Eastman, Teicholz, Sacks, and Liston (2011, p. 16).
8　An image of the numeral "5" (in jpeg format, for example), does not allow the number 5 to be used in computation. As a representation of the number 5, the image is not computable. By contrast, representing the number 5 by its binary equivalent 101 is computable.
9　Eastman et al. (2011, p. 17).
10　Eastman et al. (2011,p. 99 ff.).
11　See http://www.wbdg.org/resources/cobie.php.
12　Carpo (2011, p. 26 ff.).
13　Current AIA contract documents incorporate the notion of Levels of Development (LOD) which are used in the contract to specify how much information will be included about a given system at selected benchmark points in the project.
14　Designers can also be more involved in construction with the use of computer-numerically controlled (CNC) tools, as discussed in Chapter 4.
15　Examples include Construction Manager–General Contractor (CMGC), Construction Manager At-Risk, design–build and Integrated Project Delivery (IPD).
16　For a complete description of the principles of IPD, see American Institute of Architects; AIA California Council (2007).
17　Cuff (1991, p. 46).
18　As pointed out earlier, "drawings" generated from a BIM are a view of information and not drawings in the traditional sense.
19　Whether to accommodate established work patterns or to meet contractual requirements, architects often force BIM projects to conform to the traditional phases, but it is a distraction and a waste of time to filter BIM data to meet the customary norms for each phase. Owner–architect agreements are now available that dispense with these phases and use Levels of Development

(LOD) instead to specify what information should be included in the architectural BIM at various stages of a project (see AIA document E-202, 2013).

20 For further information on BIM servers, see Eastman et al. (2011, p. 136 ff.).

21 These capabilities are currently largely unrealized due to the wide variety of owners' information requirements. Providing an owner with a copy of a BIM raises difficult risk management issues that owner-architect agreements are beginning to address.

22 Finau and Lee (n.d.).

23 Ibbitson (2013).

24 Negro (2012).

4

COMPUTATIONAL DESIGN

The creative figure will be both the designer of algorithms and the interpreter of their outcomes.

(Peter Weibel)[1]

BIM shifts the focus of building design from the final result to the process of designing and constructing it. The organization of this process is altered in a manner that prioritizes performance criteria as design goals. While this may well affect the form of a particular building, BIM can in principle be used to construct whatever form an architect may envision.[2] As a tool, BIM has little effect on form except as it may affect some aspect of performance. By contrast, computational design is directly concerned with the generation of form. It refers to certain techniques that use computation to design, visualize, analyze and even construct buildings. Computation (as opposed to computerization) involves methods that produce new information from input data rather than merely storing and organizing it.[3] For architecture, this involves a digital model whose components are geometric objects. The form of these objects is generated by a computer based on its programming. Unlike a BIM object that carries its own geometric definition, the geometric definition of a computational design object resides in a program that generates it. Whereas BIM stores and manipulates a wide variety of information types, the primary purpose of computational design model is to create and analyze shapes. Computational design platforms therefore have more powerful ways of describing three-dimensional geometry than do BIM tools.[4]

Computational design in architecture owes much of its interest to its ability to facilitate the realization of its models as physical objects. At smaller scales, this is accomplished by CAD-CAM (computer-aided design/computer-aided manufacturing) techniques or 3D printing. CAD-CAM uses output from the designer's computer to drive computer numerically controlled (CNC) fabrication machinery (Figures 4.1, 4.2). 3D printing creates objects by depositing thin layers of some material in

FIGURE 4.1 A CNC plasma cutter capable of cutting sheets of metal as thick as 1/4″.

Source: Devaes/ CC BY-SA 3.0.

FIGURE 4.2 A CNC pipe cutter/bender used in fabricating piping and conduit with accuracy sufficient to allow their installation on site with no errors.

Steve Brown Photography/CC BY-SA 3.0.

FIGURE 4.3 A 3D printer works by depositing successive thin layers of some material, usually a plastic, building up complex three-dimensional objects.

Source: Ben Osteen/CC BY 2.0.

FIGURE 4.4
A 3D-printed flute.

Source: Jeanbaptisteparis/ CC BY 2.0.

successive passes (Figures 4.3, 4.4). At larger scales, the computer model can be used to create full-scale templates and other documents from which a building or object can be built by others. Technologies are being developed that will allow the fabrication of larger physical components directly from digital files, such as by 3D printing concrete.[5]

Computational design is rapidly increasing the range of feasible build-able shapes. In the past decade, architects have taken to this like kids in a sandbox, resulting in a welter of exotic objects featuring multiply curved surfaces and other previously impossible formal gestures that often display great virtuosity in their construction (Figures 4.5, 4.6). As a result,

FIGURES 4.5 AND 4.6 Gehry Partners LLC, Experience Music Project (c. 2000). Exterior detail (above) and interior view (opposite). This project made early use of computer-numerically controlled (CNC) machinery in the fabrication of structural steel as well as the skin panels. The curved structural steel bends visible in the lower/right hand image were fabricated by cutting the webs with a CNC plasma cutter and separately bending the flanges with a CNC variable-pressure roller to conform to the curvature of the web.

Jon Stockton/CC BY-SA 3.0; Joe Mabel/CC BY-SA 3.0.

computational design has often been associated with novel, curvilinear building forms and criticized as arbitrary and lacking any apparent motivation other than the whim of the designer. In spite of protests to the contrary,[6] many writings on computational design evince a belief in the inherent value of novelty. The ability of computational processes to generate unforeseen results is valued by some authors for itself:

> The power of computation, which involves vast quantities of calculations, combinatorial analysis, randomness, or recursion, to name a few, point out to [sic] new "thought" processes that may have not ever occurred to the human mind. These "idea generators" which are based on computational schemes have a profound ability not only to expand the limits of human imagination but also to point out the potential limitations of the human mind.[7]

This point of view is not confined to computational design. Experiments in architectural form have often been defended on the grounds that new architectural forms are required because the conditions under which architecture is created, used and interpreted have changed, or simply that the purpose of architecture is to conduct a search for new forms (Figure 4.7). To the extent that such "arguments" underwrite experiments in form,

FIGURE 4.7   Golden Terraces shopping mall in Warsaw.

Source: Mateusz Wlodarczyk/GFDL.

computational design is merely a computer game masquerading as architectural research. Used more purposefully, computational design can be a means of investigating genuine architectural problems and become a potent architectural tool. Many uses of computational design achieve

FIGURE 4.8 ICD/ITKE University of Stuttgart, Bilder Pavilion (2010). Overall view of the pavilion.

Source: ©ICD/ITKE University of Stuttgart.

FIGURE 4.9 ICD/ITKE University of Stuttgart, Bilder Pavilion (2010). Interior view of the pavilion.

Source: ©ICD/ITKE University of Stuttgart.

FIGURE 4.10
ICD/ITKE University of Stuttgart, Bilder Pavilion (2010). Detail of the interwoven plywood pieces.

Source: ©ICD/ITKE University of Stuttgartt

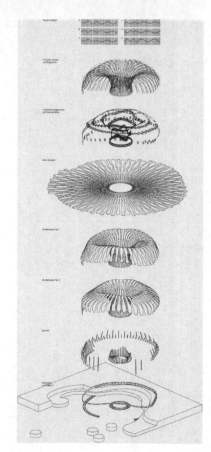

FIGURE 4.11 ICD/ITKE University of Stuttgart, Bilder Pavilion (2010). The controlling geometry generates the plywood component pieces. This process takes account of the material properties of the plywood used.

Source: ©ICD/ITKE University of Stuttgart.

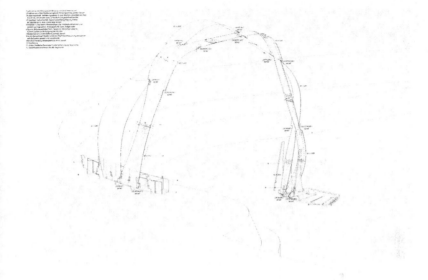

FIGURE 4.12 ICD/ITKE University of Stuttgart, Bilder Pavilion (2010). A pair pf plywood components showing their configurations and interweaving.

Source: ©ICD/ITKE University of Stuttgart.

significance as the products of new methods of design, visualization, analysis and construction made possible by the transfer of geometric operations from the human designer to the computer. These methods can solve problems with simultaneous constraints imposed by site, materials, construction techniques and geometric configuration (Figures 4.8, 4.9, 4.10, 4.11, 4.12). In addition, its pragmatic applications in the building industry continue to expand the repertoire of feasible building forms and open up new construction methods (Figures 4.13, 4.14).

There are three broad categories of computational design. The differences among them reflect different ways of creating and editing shapes in the computer. In the first type, the designer creates shapes manually, as it were, one at a time. An intuitive graphical interface allows the designer to control complex mathematical processes that generate shapes. This method is useful for describing, analyzing, and fabricating complex shapes the designer has already determined to a large extent, and to overcome the difficulty of representing them. One of its limitations is the difficulty of editing such a model; to implement changes, each component

FIGURE 4.13 SHoP Architects, Barclays Center (c. 2012). Detail.
Source: © David Kutz.

FIGURE 4.14 SHoP Architects, Barclays Center (c. 2012). Façade detail.
Source: © David Kutz.

must be moved or reshaped individually by the designer. This makes exploring variations slow and laborious. This method is also prone to willful shape-making. Unless some kind of discipline is imposed on the design process, it is easy for designers to be seduced by the shapes they see on their monitors and proceed on the basis of the visual appeal of these virtual artifacts. Lacking both precedent and a clear generative process, the resulting shapes can be difficult to justify as architectural form and may give rise to the kind of criticism mentioned above. Yet another limitation of this process is that each model describes only a single object. This sounds natural, but the more powerful uses of computational design rely on its ability to describe whole classes of objects by means of a single parametric model.

This capability is the defining characteristic of the second category, called *parametric design*. Here, shapes are generated from a set of values (parameters) and computational procedures (algorithms) that characterize the formal characteristics of a shape. The designer's task shifts from one of visualizing an object directly to formulating relationships that will generate an object. The critical difference between traditional design processes and parametric design is that, while traditional design is "top-down" (i.e. the designer begins by envisioning a form), parametric design is "bottom-up", generating form from abstract relationships.

> Rather than the designer creating the design solution (by direct manipulation) as in conventional design tools, the idea [of parametric design] is that the designer establishes relationships by which parts connect, builds up a design using these relationships and edits the relationships by observing and selecting from the results produced . . .[8]

The parametric designer is a computer programmer: he begins by defining a set of parameters and writing a set of algorithms that will determine a shape. These initial definitions chosen by the designer embody his ideas about the conditions the shape must meet; he leaves it to the computer to find a shape that meets these conditions. The role of the designer as an interpreter of computer-generated designs now emerges. Once a shape has been generated, the designer evaluates it by means of performance simulations as well as visually. By inserting different values for various parameters, or by modifying the algorithmic structure, the designer varies the shape generated by the model. This can be done by direct keyboard input, moving visible anchor points with a mouse, using graphical "sliders," or automatically by means of a script. To simplify the job of revision, parametric design usually proceeds from rough models based on a relatively small number of parameters and rules to more detailed models as the design becomes more resolved. Parametric designers use a strategy of deferral that "commits to a network of relations and defers commitment to specific location and details."[9]

The third category of computational design, called *algorithmic design*, is a special type of parametric design. In general parametric design, the parametric system produces a single shape by a single execution of the algorithmic system. In algorithmic design, an algorithmic system is executed many times to arrive at a number of shapes by means of recursion. In a recursive process, the results of one execution of the process (a generation) are used as the input for the next (Figure 4.15).

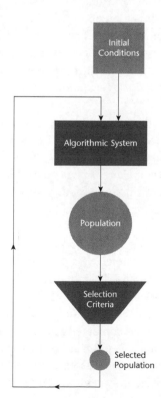

FIGURE 4.15 Diagram of a recursive algorithmic system.

Source: © Author.

An algorithmic design model has three principal parts:

1   A parametric description of a material system that expresses the relevant properties of material and construction/fabrication methods to be used, along with a geometric schema to guide the development of the spatial development of the system.

2   Analytic procedures to assess how well each resulting system meets specified *fitness criteria*. The designer selects certain criteria the design must meet, such as an energy performance benchmark. A separate computer program that evaluates systems according to each of these criteria is provided and linked to the parametric model.

3   Computational processes that generate virtual objects from the parametric description of the material system.[10]

An algorithmic design process begins much like a parametric process. The designer works at the level of the algorithmic system, not of that the object. He writes a set of algorithms that express the properties of a building system (precast concrete panels, for example) and the design requirements the building must satisfy. After each execution of the algorithmic system, the resulting shapes are tested to find those that best satisfy the design requirements. These are then used as the input for the next run. The process is repeated, often thousands of times.

Algorithmic design introduces *population thinking* into architectural design. Rather than refining a single design in pursuit of a unique, ideal solution, algorithmic design operates on a large number of possible solutions (a population) and selects and refines these to arrive at a solution (Figure 4.16). In a well-designed algorithmic process, a point comes at which further recursions yield progressively less improvement in the solutions' ability to meet the selection criteria: the recursive process converges on a single solution. This property is called *stability*. The form of a stable solution cannot be predicted by the designer. It is *emergent*, meaning that it has been produced from the conditions of the design problem itself.

There are clear similarities between algorithmic design and biological evolution under natural selection. The computer code that generates the architectural form can be likened to the genetic code that generates biological form. Testing members of a population according to design criteria is analogous to natural selection. Like organisms, the objects

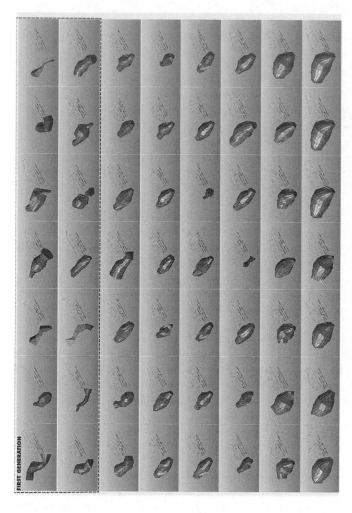

FIGURE 4.16 Objects describing the design space of the Galapagos project by John Locke as it develops through successive generations.

Source: © John Locke.

that result from algorithmic design are naturally suited by a process of selection to their environments as expressed in the fitness criteria. In both realms, form is not primary, but the secondary result of the selection process.

The Fourth Geometry

Computational design is based on transferring geometric operations from humans to computers. Since computers perform these operations in fundamentally different ways than do humans, the meaning of geometry in architecture is transformed by this transfer. It adds a new chapter to the history of geometry in architecture—a fourth type of architectural geometry in addition to the three Evans identifies—that is in no way tied to representation in the sense expressed in Chapter 1. This new type of geometry, which we may call *virtual*, is proper to computers.

Human geometry is based on concepts. Euclid built his geometry on a set of concepts which he called "Common Notions" or axioms. These are ideas that we intuitively feel to be true, such as "the whole is greater than the part" (Common Notion 5).[11] Concepts like this are universal; they are true under any circumstances. Humans search for conceptual relationships, valid in a wide range of instances, and apply them to specific situations. Our minds grasp simple geometric forms as concepts. Even a very rough drawing of a circle will evoke the concept of a circle in our minds. Computers, on the other hand, do not use concepts; they perform calculations on quantities.[12] To use computers to perform geometric operations, humans had to translate concepts into programs that *produce a shape* that corresponds to a concept. Thus we say that computers "plot" a shape, i.e., they calculate a series of points that approximate it when appropriately displayed.[13] A shape in a computer is entirely defined by the process by which it is generated, i.e. they are defined *operationally*. As computational geometry researcher Bruce Naylor puts it, "Computation is constructive mathematics." He goes on to say: "[T]he primary measure of value [of computation] is not provability per se (as much as we might want error-free programs), but rather performance and accuracy."[14]

Virtual geometry cannot provide proofs of universal relationships as Euclidean geometry does; it is tied to specific instances. Provability requires working with concepts in order to show that a given relationship is true in general, independent of specific instances and numerical values. Computers cannot do this (yet). What they do is to perform arithmetic operations very fast. The criterion of accuracy Naylor mentions reflects the fact that the representation of a concept by a series of numerical calculations (i.e. a construction) is always approximate. This approximation can be made as close as desired, but greater accuracy comes at the cost of longer computation times. Formal simplicity has little meaning in computerized operations; the same operations that generate a sphere can generate an arbitrarily curved surface almost as easily.[15]

What happens to geometry with the displacement of representation by simulation is twofold: First, the epistemological function of traditional geometry disappears. Geometry no longer gives us the measure of the world, no longer links our thought to external reality. Second, geometric operations become opaque. We design or borrow a system of algorithms, hit "Run" and await the results. What happens in between is in effect the working of an alien mind.

Whereas the objects of traditional geometry are either ideal or physical, the objects of computational geometry are virtual. A virtual object is a fundamentally different type of entity than either ideas or objects. They exist only in the computer and lie entirely outside of human experience. Humans cannot think with virtual objects; we must rely on sensible artifacts (seeing display images, handling 3D prints, etc.) that the computer generates from them. These artifacts are in effect simulations of simulations, algorithmically generated experiences of algorithmically simulated geometric operations.

In order to perform geometric operations with computers, new ways of describing geometry were invented by computer scientists. Computer-based descriptions (or "representations") of geometry employ a variety of techniques to construct a form by joining small pieces together. By constructing a shape from ever smaller pieces, it can be approximated to whatever degree of precision (or resolution) is desired. The only limitation is the increasing amount of time required by the calculations as the pieces become more numerous. Utter precision would require the shape to be composed of an infinite number of pieces, requiring an infinite amount of time to compute, so in practice some degree of approximation must be accepted. The calculations involved would be impossible for an unaided human to carry out in a reasonable amount of time. Very complex shapes generated this way can be used in a design process without

perceptibly affecting speed and immediacy, provided the required resolution is not too great.

Before we apply the word "form" to the shapes generated by computational design, an expanded definition of the term is needed. In its
traditional sense, form entails a relationship between an object of perception and an ideal order to which it corresponds in some way. Form
exists in the mind. Plato used the terms Form and Idea interchangeably.
Objects in the world of perception approximate forms but remain only an
imperfect embodiment of them. In the realm of geometry, the "ideal"
forms are those that had the highest degree of symmetry, making them
easily held in the mind (Figure 4.17). This quality does not in general
apply to computationally generated shapes. Yet it is undeniable that there
are some that convey a sense of order though we are hard pressed to hold
it in our minds as we do Euclidean forms (Figure 4.18).

Many kinds of mathematical order are not apparent to us unless they
are presented spatially. Often a visual display of a mathematical system
is needed in order for us to perceive the order within it (Figure 4.19). The
techniques of computational design have enormously expanded the range
of types of mathematical order architectural form can embody. Although
the forms produced by computational design are generally unfamiliar,
they are the result of mathematical processes and are therefore ordered in
some fashion. This is what gives rise to the sense of order we feel in their
presence. The idea of form, applied to the products of computational
design, shifts from order that arises from the prior experience of the

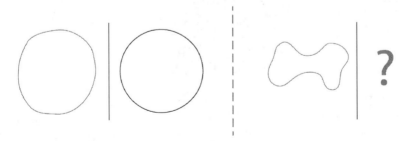

FIGURE 4.17 Real figures can be considered forms if they approximate an
ideal form (left). Otherwise, they are considered shapes rather than form
(right).

Source: © Author

FIGURE 4.18 Vlad Tenu, *Minimal Complexity* (2012). The overall form of this sculpture has a high degree order without obvious basis in our experience. The order is mathematical. The artist says, "The constraints in the creative process refer to the play with symmetry planes—following similar principles of triply periodic minimal surfaces."

Source: © Vlad Tenu

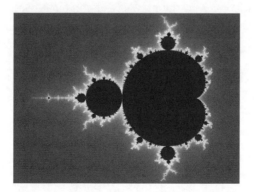

FIGURE 4.19 The Mandelbrot set displays many levels of order immediately apparent to the eye when appropriately displayed. This order is unintelligible in other forms, such as the algebraic formula that generates this image: $Z_{n+1} = Z_n^2 + C$.

Source: Wolfgang Beyer/CC BY-SA 3.0.

observer to a broader notion of *form as immediately perceived or intuited order*. In other words, computational design introduces new types of order not based on experience.

Parametric/algorithmic design raises fascinating questions about the possible existence of a mathematical structure underlying intuited form. If such forms do not arise in our experience, where do they come from? What could the meaning of such a form be? Is there a mathematical structure behind all such intuited spatial order and is it possible to find it? Does such a structure represent a "limit-form" as ideal geometric forms do in Euclidean geometry? The design of the 8 Spruce Street (formerly the Beekman Tower) project in New York City by Gehry Partners LLP highlights these questions (Figure 4.20). The final design of the exterior form was based on a physical model that was manually digitized, producing a set of points in space that could be connected in the computer by lines to give a rough profile of the envelope. Consisting of a set of unrelated, discrete points, this digital model could not easily be used to refine the design or to analyze its properties. To permit rapid analysis and easily explore design variations, a mathematical description of the shape of the envelope was needed. The general method was to find parameters and rules interrelating these parameters to produce a family of surfaces that would share the desired formal qualities of the original shape, a process called *parameterization*. Finding such a description must have been an arduous process, since the goal was to mathematically express formal ideas that were only implicit in the physical model. The parametric model allowed the shape to be modified as a whole, rather than point-by-point. It also defined the surface in such a way as to enable analyses to be performed. One use of it was to subdivide the façade into panels that met dimensional constraints imposed by their fabrication. These panels were then further refined to minimize the number of doubly-curved panels to reduce their cost (Figure 4.21). The governing criterion was always that the shape satisfy the designer's formal intentions as expressed in the initial model.

FIGURES 4.20 AND 4.21 Gehry Partners LLC, 8 Spruce Street (formerly Beekman Tower, c. 2012). Full-scale mockup of a section of the exterior wall.

Source: joevare/CC BY-ND 2.0.

Computation as a Medium

Computation is the medium proper to parametric and algorithmic design. It affects design in ways analogous to the effects of physical media on drawing and construction. Computation has definite properties that the architect/programmer must understand and work with rather than against, a kind of conceptual "grain." These properties favor certain approaches to a design problem and penalize or disallow others. There is a craft associated with computation, requiring an understanding of this medium and long practice to master it. However, this medium requires very different modes of thought than traditional design media or even non-parametric digital design tools. Programming makes use of different cognitive skills than traditional design. First, programming involves learning languages and acquiring the ability to express oneself freely in them. The expression of ideas in language is never transparent. Any language shapes an idea it is used to express; casting design ideas into the terms required by a computer language cannot but affect those ideas. Computer languages differ from natural ones in that they are designed. This has the advantage of making their rules clear and exception-free, but it forces their users to be precise and explicit in their thinking. Any language has rules that cannot be broken without losing the meaning of what is being "said." However, unlike human beings who have considerable ability to interpret (and make creative use of) faulty or ambiguous utterances, computers have no tolerance for errors in parsing a program. Imprecise computer code does not produce evocative images as an imprecise sketch might; it simply doesn't work. A high degree of precision is required in a computational design process from the outset. This contrasts strongly with a drawing-based design process in which vagueness and ambiguity are essential. They allow the designer to explore and develop partially formed ideas, or even give rise to new ones. Every decision taken presents new possibilities which the process proposes for exploration. Premature foreclosure of design possibilities is one of the classic mistakes that design teachers caution their students to avoid. A drawing-based design process moves cautiously from the vague to the definite, working at each step to understand the full implications of the decision being made. In computation, every step must be expressed precisely in terms of code. There is no possibility of ambiguity.

Second, computation is an opaque medium for the creation of form. Rather than directly manipulating form as drawing does, computational designers create form at a remove by writing code that in turn generates form. The designer's task is to design an algorithmic process that reflects the design problem and leads to a stable solution, not to envision the solution directly. The resulting inability to predict formal outcomes is a virtue in the minds of some algorithmic designers who seek emergent, self-organized form that could not be envisioned beforehand by a designer.[16] The extent to which designers can develop an intuition about relationships between code and form is not clear yet. These relationships will surely become more transparent as young architects emerge from a background in which coding is a common skill.[17] It is possible that future architects may see form in code as readily as we now see it in drawings, as some musicians can hear a piece of music by reading a score. Even if this comes to pass, however, the cognitive operation involved will be dramatically different than that involved in drawing.

Finally, as a design medium, computation requires systems thinking.[18] A system in this sense is an entity whose behavior can only be explained by interactions among its parts, not as the aggregate of the behaviors of the parts themselves. Buildings are systems. Windows, for example, affect heating and cooling loads. It is a commonplace that design should integrate the various components of a building to create something "greater than the sum of its parts." But truly thinking holistically about a design is very difficult with traditional methods, for the reason that the interactions among its components are many, complex, and interrelated. It is precisely the interactions among building components that are at the heart of a parametric/algorithmic model. The foregrounding of interactions rather than objects represents a significant departure from traditional design thinking, and designers must learn to approach a project in these terms in parametric and algorithmic design.

Understanding form in terms of relationships rather than objects is not our natural mode of perception. Objects present themselves directly to our perception; we perceive *things* and only subsequently may we discover relationships among them. We understand objects metrically, that is, we measure them with our eyes and hands and relate them to the size of our bodies. Objects have material qualities. While we can certainly imagine shapes without any such qualities, these are abstractions from our experience, which is of tangible objects composed of materials with texture, color, hardness, etc. Relationships, on the other hand, are abstract by definition. A relationship, such as intersection, can apply to any pair

FIGURE 4.22 The abstract idea of intersection can be applied to disparate sets such as numbers and animals.

Source: © Author.

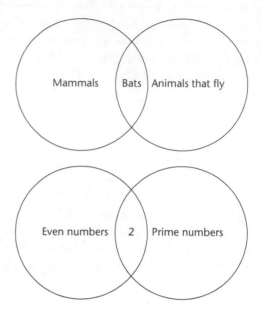

of objects. What the objects are is irrelevant. Intersection is a concept that we can apply to sets of any kind of entity, material or ideal (Figure 4.22). The need to think of form in terms of relationships required by para-metric/algorithmic design is a sharp break with how we have conceived form until now.

Thinking of a design in terms of parameters and relationships among them means that the process is no longer conceived in concrete spatial terms. The two dimensions of a drawing are spatial, two of the three in which objects represented by a drawing exist. The reduction of three dimensions to two is accomplished by some form of projection, a geometric operation and therefore spatial, so that the space in which the object exists and the space represented by the drawing can both be of the same kind. A parametric model may describe something that exists in three-dimensional geometric space, but in terms of the generalized notion of space mentioned above. Instead of the three spatial coordinates (x, y, z), the model is characterized by a set of parameters that can represent many different characteristics of the object, some geometric (length, radius, etc.), some material (weight, tensile strength, transparency), and some abstract (intersection priority, hierarchical position, display color).

The configuration and characteristics of any part of a model are given by a set of parameter values. Any set of independent parameters that completely specifies objects in a model can be seen in mathematical terms as the *basis* of an abstract space, akin to the (x, y, z) basis of three-dimensional geometric space. Just as any geometric figure can be completely defined by functions of (x, y, z), an object in a parametric model can be defined by functions of its parameters $(p_1, p_2, . . . p_n)$. This abstract space is called the *phase space* or *state space*. It is in terms of such a space that the parametric designer thinks. Computer code will translate the phase space into three-dimensional geometric space, plus additional dimensions for non-spatial attributes of the object. If designers wish to anticipate the effects of manipulations in phase space on the object they are designing, they must learn to translate phase space into geometric space. In many cases of algorithmic design, the spatial object cannot be foreseen from its phase space description.

Parametric design is thus carried out in an abstract space whose relationship to geometric space is often not clear to the designer. The homology (similarity of form) between a representational artifact such as a drawing and the object being designed is gone. There are two possible benefits of thinking about design this way. First, by encoding rules for the generation of form rather than a form *per se*, whole classes of objects that share specified properties can be generated. This allows design to become a process of selection and modification. Common characteristics encoded in the parametric model can ensure that the members of a class all meet certain design requirements. These solutions can then be tested for their performance according to other criteria (energy use, for example) and modifications made to try to improve their performance. A much larger set of possible solutions can be explored in this way compared to a traditional process in which only a few alternatives can be considered due to the time needed to create and analyze each alternative with traditional methods.

The second benefit stems from a critique of traditional design processes. In this view, prioritizing form by designing it directly turns design on its head: instead of searching for a form that satisfies the project's requirements, as is usually done, the requirements themselves drive the form. This is the premise of algorithmic design. The form emerges from a complex of constraints on and interrelationships among parameters. The designer's lack of direct control over the form neutralizes any preconceptions and allows unforeseen, novel solutions to arise. The designer's inability to predict the spatial configuration of the result is precisely the point of this process.

Through the device of designing in phase space, parametric/algorithmic design offers the ability to rapidly generate solutions to design problems and circumvent limitations of the designer's imagination. These techniques relocate the designer's work *to the design of the algorithmic structure* and *the critique of its products*. These are the loci of creativity in parametric/algorithmic design. They require the new skills described above and have profound consequences for how architecture is thought and experienced.

Form and Intention

The history of architecture is replete with theories about the relationship between architectural form and human thought, but nearly all assume that a form can be understood as a direct expression of the designer's intentions, that every aspect of a form is (or should be) the result of a conscious decision on the part of the designer. Broadening of the notion of form as implied by parametric and algorithmic design entails a re-examination of this assumption. In parametric and algorithmic design, the expression of design intentions is not direct but expressed in computer code that plays an active role in creating the final form so that the outcome is often unforeseeable to the designer.[19] The final design can be viewed in such cases as the result of a dual agency—a *hybrid subject* of design comprising human and computer rather than as the direct expression of the human designer's intentions. Nicolas Negroponte described this new subject in these terms:

> We shall . . . treat the problem [of how machines might assist in the design process] as the intimate association of two dissimilar species: man and machine; and two dissimilar processes: design and computation. We shall further define our concern as the acquaintanceship of two intelligent systems, the architect and the Architecture Machine. By virtue of ascribing intelligence to an artefact or to the artificial, the partnership is not one of master (smart, leader) and slave (dumb, follower), but rather of two associates which each have the potential for self-improvement.[20]

The designer's role in the parametric/algorithmic design process is first to create (i.e. program) the computational structure which generates the designs that will emerge from the computational process. This structure consists of code that specifies the parameters, their constraints and the algorithms that relate them. This code is the most basic level at which the designer's ideas are expressed. These are not limited to the formal, but can embody the full range of intentions normally associated with design: "An algorithm is not only a computer implementation, a series of lines of code in a program, or a language, it is also a theoretical construct with deep philosophical, social, design and artistic repercussions."[21]

In order to be sufficiently rich to generate a wide range of actual instances, this structure must be topological, that is, related to the connectivity of its parts rather than quantitative measures such as size.[22] However, this structure alone is not sufficient to generate specific forms. To do so, the designer must also specify the initial conditions (parameter values), the starting point of the computational process. Very different forms can result from the same computational structure given different initial conditions. The structure and initial conditions embody the designer's fundamental choices that will shape the final design. The combination of structure and initial conditions must generate sufficiently rich populations of designs for the process to yield unforeseen, stable results.[23] This is a complex design problem in itself, requiring the designer to understand the properties of computational processes that create productive systems.

Another crucial decision made by the designer is the selection of fitness criteria for winnowing populations between iterations of the algorithmic system. These criteria are properties or characteristics the designer wishes the design to have. They are often measures of the design's interaction with its physical environment (e.g. energetic, thermodynamic, visual, material, etc.), but other less tangible factors can be used as well. The choice of fitness criteria is clearly of the greatest importance in shaping the final design. Through the choice of these criteria, designers express many of the values they wish to bring to the project.

Once a system is created, the designer begins to evaluate and modify the resulting forms. This is a crucial but often unacknowledged part of computational design and an essential if fraught part of any design process. The insights gained from unselfconscious thought (intuition) applied in this situation can be invaluable, but there is a fine line separating true insights from arbitrary manipulations that obscure rather than advance the design. In traditional design, such ideas directly affect the design itself, but here they must express themselves indirectly, in computational terms.[24] It may be possible to train one's design intuition to work in terms of the effects of computational systems on form,[25] but it is easier to experiment with different initial conditions and variations on the algorithmic structure. In computational design, the designer must make the initial intentions explicit in creating the algorithmic structure and selection of fitness criteria, while a traditional design may leave these vague, to be clarified during design.

The products of computational design demand to be interpreted on different bases than traditionally designed objects. First, they cannot be understood as direct expressions of the designer's intentions. Any given feature is more likely to be the result of a computational process than a conscious decision of the designer. The observer is unlikely to be able to trace the designer's intentions through their computational expression to their effects on the form. The influences of the workings of computational processes on the final object are not predictable to the designer, let alone the observer. This unpredictability is an inherent and crucial part of the process. Deviation, translation, the unforeseeable, the alien are among its properties. Second, because computational geometry is not grounded in our everyday experience, its forms cannot have symbolic significance. So far, most interpretations of these objects have regarded them as "sculptural," at best an attempt to fit them into a familiar and comfortably vague category. But this is not very enlightening. The consequences of parametric/algorithmic design processes in architecture are radical and their reception must come to grips with this fact.

Emergence and Meaning

Many academic practitioners of algorithmic design call attention to similarities between algorithmic design and natural evolution. Some see it as a way to create buildings that are inherently environmentally responsive by methods similar to those that adapt organisms so perfectly to their environments:

> The perfection and variety of natural forms are the result of relentless experimentation of evolution. By means of profligate prototyping and the ruthless rejection of flawed experiments, nature

has evolved a rich biodiversity of interdependent species of plants and animals that are in balance with their environment. While vernacular architecture might occasionally share some of these characteristics, the vast majority of buildings in our contemporary environment most certainly do not.[26]

By this account, algorithmic design acquires an ethical motivation. By basing the design process on environmental criteria and allowing buildings to emerge from them, environmental responsiveness is installed as a value at the very core of architectural design. The design process is now conceived on the basis of environmental responsiveness, embodying a digital simulation of nature's own processes that ensure the adaptation of organisms to their environments. Form emerges from the requirement that buildings become part of their ecosystems.

There are, however, significant differences between natural selection and algorithmic design. One is that random genetic variation is but one strategy available to algorithmic designers for seeding successive generations. Furthermore, selection criteria are employed differently. In nature, survival is binary: an organism either lives or dies. If it dies, none of its genetic material can be inherited by future generations. Algorithmic design allows a range of adaptivity, degrees of survival as it were, that permit some variation among selected designs, leaving open the possibility that some may give rise to more successful solutions in later generations. Most importantly, designers can devise criteria that select for qualities they consider desirable that are not physical, but esthetic or humane. More generally, emergence implies very different bases for the significance of architectural form. Traditionally, this has been understood as the direct expression of thought, occasioned and mediated by natural conditions and cultural influences. It has been interpreted according to expectations of unified intention and expressive coherence. By contrast, emergent form created by (or arrived at) by algorithmic design is not the direct creation of a human mind, but the product of thought expressed through an alien process that renders it unrecognizable. In spite of the similarities of the design process to impersonal natural processes, such form is not the result of an autonomous process. The hand of the designer is everywhere in it, but it is impossible to see precisely what effects it has had. Such a form's significance lies largely in its satisfaction of the requirements of its internal conditions and environment, but the connections between these and form, like the intentions of the designer, cannot be directly apprehended. This demands new attitudes on the part of both designer and observer.

One possibility is to see the intention of and response to such objects as emergent in its own right:

> [E]mergence is not only a property of pattern-formation or physical self-organization. Emergence is also a factor in behavior and function . . . Novelty arises not only in formal arrangement (a typical desire in conventional computerized approaches), but is more fruitfully applied in the realization of multiple behavioral capacities— ones not initially imagined during the genesis of the process.[27]

Thus, intention and response are to be produced, like the object itself, as a result of the process. To some this may sound like an abdication of the designer's role or a rationalization of limitations of the process. It may seem to some like the royal road to empty expressionism. But by his very adoption of this method, a designer declares a very strong intention: to have his design received without the possibility of its being understood as an expression of his intentions. Perhaps there are as yet undiscovered ways of interpreting objects made this way. It is incumbent upon algorithmic designers to demonstrate what these may be.

Performativity

Parametric/algorithmic design is inherently performance-based in that the characteristics of a solution being sought must be explicitly stated in computational terms, as parameters, properties or selection criteria. At first blush, the use of a computer to determine the characteristics of a design would seem to require that these be described in terms that can be evaluated quantitatively. This would indeed be strictly performative and is in fact how these techniques are often used, particularly in current construction practice. However, there are ways of using computation, particularly in algorithmic design, that avoid this situation. The nature of algorithmic systems allows design goals to be approached in many ways, and this flexibility provides the designer a substantial degree of freedom. The architect can use selection criteria that reflect many different kinds of concerns, not only the performative. The designer's direct intervention at various stages of the design process allows non-performative judgments to affect the final outcome. Finally, computation does not always produce deterministic results. While an individual algorithm gives a determined output, a system of several algorithms carried out recursively can produce an essentially non-deterministic result.[28] Emergent form is found by procedures of this kind. Nevertheless, parametric/algorithmic design is often used in current practice to optimize a design's configuration with respect to such factors as cost, energy use, solar gain, zoning envelope compliance, viewshed, and shadow casting. Such analyses sometimes provide functional justifications for seemingly extravagant forms. There is a risk of bad faith here. Portraying a design as functionally motivated both frees the architect from criticism of other values that may underlie it, and lends function undeserved prestige as its basis. Parametric/algorithmic design can thus promote a paradoxical combination of functionalism and expressionism.

Bodily Engagement

A common criticism of digital design tools is their failure to engage the body in any significant way.[29] Much has already been said here about the importance of the bodily engagement provided by drawing in establishing connections between design and both the construction and experience of buildings. It is certain that, in its current form, this criticism of computational design is justified. The question is: to what extent is the lack of bodily engagement a technical shortcoming that can be corrected, and to what extent is it a fundamental property of this medium?

The current interface of mouse, keyboard, and monitor leaves a great deal to be desired from this point of view. In the first place, the designer's relationship to the design is almost entirely visual, and then only through a window that takes up only a small portion of his visual field. Thanks to television and computers, we are accustomed to tuning out most of our visual field and immersing ourselves in small windows. In an architectural design medium, though, we need to be aware of this habit and the distortions it creates in our perception of space. The equating of visual experience with experience *in toto* is another habit we owe to our cultural heritage which has privileged vision above the other senses.[30] Current simulations depend upon and reinforce this prejudice. Vision is the furthest-reaching of our senses, giving us the ability to take in vast spaces, to name and order enormous numbers of objects through their appearance and spatial relationships, even at remote distances. This dominance promotes an instrumental relationship with our environment.[31] Without the more intimate relationships created by the other senses that operate at much closer range, vision detaches us from our surroundings and limits our engagement with the world. Vision thus dominates our surroundings, bringing everything within its huge sweep into a totality centered on the viewer. The instrumental attitude towards the world associated with vision is particularly conducive to technology which also sees the world as material available for our use, "to hand," in Heidegger's phrase. Such a relationship stands in direct opposition to the ethos of environmental responsibility that is becoming more prevalent in our society, particularly in architecture.

The current interface also barely engages the body in its manipulation. A mouse is obviously a poor substitute for the infinite subtleties of hand drawing. Computers interpret mouse inputs precisely even when hand motions reflect a designer's uncertainty. The irregularities of its movement are smoothed over by software that has been told in advance what kind of shape (line, circle, spline, etc.) the user intends to make. A mouse is only sensitive to its location; factors such as pressure, speed, angle, and lead hardness that affect the mark of a pencil have no effect on a mouse. Also, much of the mouse's movement has nothing to do with defining forms, but rather performing software-related actions such as selecting tools. And, when accuracy matters, forms are defined by keyboard entries, not using the mouse at all.

Many efforts are underway to both improve the visual dimension of simulations and to extend them to the aural and the haptic. 3D prints begin to engage the body by allowing designers to handle forms and experience them through touch and visual apperception as they do traditional models. This is valuable as far as it goes, but denies designers not only direct experience with the qualities of physical media, but also the experience of planning and constructing a physical object. To make the visual experience of simulations more body-based, immersive environments are becoming more common (Figure 4.23). Another approach is the development of computer interfaces that make use of body movements to control the user's interaction with a simulation. The difficulty here is in programming the computer to identify a certain movement with a particular command. One strategy is to use a learned vocabulary of hand gestures.[32]

FIGURE 4.23 Engineers use CAVE to tour a virtual nuclear reactor, train workers, and look at alternative designs.

Source: The Idaho National Laboratory/CC BY 2.0.

Although this employs the hand in space, the gestural code can be just as artificial as mouse movements. Providing a tactile dimension to simulations is the aim of haptic technology. Simple applications of this are found in some video game controllers that vibrate or "rumble" when appropriate during the game action. More sophisticated devices are being created all the time, even simulating the sensation of turning a doorknob (Figures 4.24, 4.25).[33, 34] Even the *Star Trek* fantasy of a tangible hologram is becoming a reality.[35, 36]

Since very few architects can make use of these innovations, the limitations of the interface are extremely important in current practice. If not compensated for in some way, architects are led to accept a misleading visual simulation as the reality of the buildings they are designing. The appeal of what they see on their monitors can easily overwhelm their sense of the actual qualities the building will have. They can choose vantage points for their views that show the project to advantage even though no one will ever see the building from that point of view. They may become so fascinated by a particular visual effect of the simulation that they forget to think about what its actual impact will be on the building. And any sense of real materiality will be replaced by the visual simulation before them.

FIGURE 4.24 Reactive Grip, under development at the Haptic Lab at the University of Utah, combines a tactile feedback device (below/right) with a visual interface (above/left). The combination of the haptic feedback provided by the Reactive Grip device and the visual interface creates a realistic experience of turning the door knob and opening the door.

Source: © William Provancher.

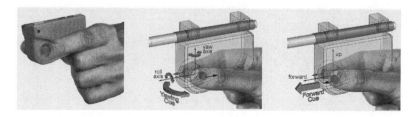

FIGURE 4.25 The haptic device creates forces in the hand that simulate resistance to turning and pushing.

Source: © William Provancher.

Notes

1 Peter Weibel, "Algorithmus und Kreativität," in *Woher Kommt das Neue? Kreativität in Wissenschaft und Kunst* (Vienna: Bohau Verlag, 2003), p. 301, quoted in Menges & Ahlquist, "Introduction" (2011, p. 26).
2 The operative phrase here is "in principle." In addition to the formal limitations imposed by current BIM software, there are other design effects that result from the natural tendency to be guided by one's tools and take the path they offer. One of the most pernicious of these is the uncritical use of default tool settings by BIM users, resulting in building elements that are not designed or even really chosen by the designer, but which offer themselves for easy adoption.
3 Menges & Ahlquist (2011, p. 10).
4 In the not-too-distant future, single tools will have both kinds of capability, but at present these two types of tools are distinct and combining them in a single design process, while possible, can be rather awkward.
5 Loughborough University; Foster + Partners; Buro Happold, 2010.
6 "[N]ovelty is impossible. It is only an illusion" (Terzides, 2006, p. 5).
7 Terzides (2006, p. 18).
8 Woodbury (2010, p. 24).
9 Woodbury (2010, p. 43).
10 Menges (2011, pp. 203–206).
11 Euclid (1956, p. 155).
12 While work is underway in the field of artificial intelligence to create conceptual understanding in computers, these have thus far proven to be far slower than numerical approaches to computational geometry. See, for example, Eklund & Haemmerle (2008).
13 We would gain a great deal of clarity about the status of computer-generated graphic artifacts if we called them "plots" instead of "drawings."
14 Naylor (2008).
15 To be more precise, there are limitations on the kinds of curves computational tools can generate, based on the continuity of the second derivative of the curve. This is not much of a limitation in practice for architecture because such shapes are not useful for buildings.
16 "[A]lgorithms can produce results for which there is no intention or prediction . . . of their behavior" (Terzides, 2006, p. 21).
17 An illustrative anecdote: A friend of mine was recently advising a freshman college student about the courses he should take. My friend asked the student whether he was thinking about learning a second language. The student replied, "I already know Python."
18 "Fundamental to computational design is the understanding of how systems, as form and as mathematical constructs, operate" (Menges & Ahlquist, 2011, p. 16).
19 Indeed, this unforeseeability is seen as a key feature of parametric/algorithmic design that allows it to expand design thinking. For example, Kostas Terzides

writes: "Algorithmic processes result from events that are often neither observable nor predictable and seem to be highly intuitive . . . In this sense, algorithmic processes become a vehicle for exploration that extends beyond the limits of perception" (2011, p. 98).

20 Negroponte (1969), quoted in Menges & Ahlquist (2011, pp. 78–85).
21 Terzides (2006, p. xiii).
22 deLanda (2002, p. 145–146).
23 Menges & Ahlquist (2011, pp. 15–16).
24 While it is of course possible for a designer to directly manipulate an algorithmically generated form, doing so would obviate the rationale of the process.
25 Miller (2012a and 2012b).
26 Frazer (2011, p. 151).
27 Menges & Ahlquist (2011, p. 24).
28 A recursive set of algorithms uses the output of the first algorithm as the input for the second and so on. The output of the last algorithm is then used as the input for the first to repeat the cycle which is iterated many times.
29 According to Pallasmaa:

> The architect moves about freely in the imagined structure . . . as if walking in a building and touching all its surfaces and sensing their materiality and texture. This is an intimacy that is surely difficult, if not impossible, to simulate through computer-aided means of modeling and simulation.
>
> (2009, p. 59)

30 Levin (1993).
31 Foucault (1979).
32 See, for example, Hsiao, Davis, & Do (2012).
33 Haptic & Embedded Mechatronics Laboratory (n.d.).
34 Provancher (2013).
35 Iwamoto, Tatezono, Hoshi, & Shinoda (2008).
36 Shinoda Lab, University of Tokyo (2009).

5
SIMULATION AND ARCHITECTURE

Having explored BIM and computational design in some detail, we are now in a position to return to the subject of effects of simulation on architectural practice. In Chapter 1, we developed the notion of simulation as a comprehensive mode of perception in which signs refer only to themselves and not to any external reality. In simulation, experience has no depth; it "points" to nothing outside itself. Simulation in this sense displaces reality by depriving signs of any reference; signs, in fact, no longer exist. Simulation as a mode of perception is much broader than specific simulations we encounter such as computer models, video games and the like. With the latter, the user chooses to engage a simulation and the displacement of reality only lasts for the time the user chooses to remain engaged. Specific simulations alone do not challenge reality; they are merely temporary alternatives to it. Simulation in the larger sense is not produced by specific simulations. Although technology, specifically electronic media, played an important role in its advent, simulation has far outstripped its technological origins. In what follows, the reader should be careful to distinguish between simulations in the restricted sense (like a video game) and simulation in the broader sense, as a mode of perception. We are concerned with how the specific simulations created by BIM and computational design engage and extend simulation as a mode of perception and the effects of this on architectural practice.

BIM and computational design create building simulations in the restricted sense. Many complex technical systems are now designed by means of such simulations: aircraft, drugs, and nuclear weapons, to name a few. In fact, architecture is very late to the party in adopting simulation as a design tool. The issues raised by simulation for architecture have little to do with the fidelity of individual simulations (how "real" they seem). The fidelity of simulations is increasing rapidly and these may well one day fulfill the fantasies of writers like William Gibson and Neal Stephenson, becoming truly indistinguishable from reality. However, the issues here concern the broad effects of simulation on the relationship between the architect and the prospective building he is designing. Media certainly play an important role in this relationship, but the media themselves—and how they are used—are the products of a larger social movement. The uses of these media both rely upon and perpetuate the larger phenomenon of simulation.

The issues raised by BIM and computational design are introduced by the useful, seemingly innocuous restricted simulations they create. These can make design and construction more efficient. The more questions that are answered during design, the more thoroughly a project is studied, the fewer problems will arise during a building's construction and operation. These simulations also help designers understand such things as energy use and construction cost, and being able to verify compliance with building codes and the spatial program. Obtaining these results rapidly so they can be immediately applied to further development adds to their utility. A design environment, such as that provided by BIM and computational design, that embraces many aspects of a building, is essential for architects.

Simulations are also pleasurable. This is especially true for designers, who love to see their ideas come to life. Part of this pleasure, which is the one of the pleasures of design itself, is creating a perfect world, perfect because we make it ourselves to conform to our desires. To be able to actually experience this world is like a dream come true.

Restricted, useful simulations bring on simulation in the broad sense due to the difficulty of interpreting a single model in two disparate ways. The inclusion of specific simulations in a model tends to cause the entire model to become simulation. It is very difficult if not impossible to regard a single model as both simulation and representation. These two modes require radically different attitudes towards their objects and are incompatible in a single individual. For the former, a model's purpose is to understand the performance of a building, to be its operational equivalent. For the latter, a model's purpose is to facilitate the exploration of ideas that manifest themselves differently in a model than in a building. The natural tendency is to treat the entire model as simulation in order to take advantage of the useful restricted simulations it can perform. One could imagine another solution, which would be for architects to use different models for performative simulation and for overall design. However, this would conflict with the architect's desire to see a project's technical, spatial, and expressive aspects holistically. Architects want a single design environment that supports all design decision-making. Furthermore, the pervasiveness of simulation in our society predisposes architects (along with everyone else) to accept simulation as reality in their work as they already do in so many aspects of their lives.

Simulation affects architecture as much in its reception as in its design. This can be seen in the emphasis placed on a building's image during the past 50 years or so. This tendency received theoretical legitimacy from Robert Venturi in his book, *Complexity and Contradiction in Architecture* (1966) and further elaboration in *Learning from Las Vegas* (1977).

FIGURE 5.1 Robert Venturi, Vanna Venturi House (1964). Architecture as language. The many violations of conventions of classical composition evident in this façade are the architectural equivalent of a poet's purposeful misuse of grammar for artistic effect.

Source: Smallbones.

Venturi's central idea was that a building's exterior functions as a sign and should therefore be thought of as a form of linguistic communication. For Venturi, the theorist and Rome Prize recipient, this involved informed, intentional violations of the conventions of architectural components and ordering systems (Figure 5.1). In the built environment at large this licensed a focus on architectural imagery. Buildings could now be signs that signaled whatever their owners wished to signal, by whatever means available. Most signs have external referents and are therefore representations. But what happened with buildings is that, in many cases, they became images with no referent, i.e. simulacra.

Reception

Architects must realize that the broad cultural phenomenon of simulation is beyond their, or anyone else's, control. They are confronted with a public that does not look at the built environment as bearing meaning as most architects understand the term. As an example of this, consider a typical contemporary mass-built single-family home (Figure 5.2). The interior is usually planned to meet the functional demands of the daily

FIGURE 5.2 A typical suburban tract house: an image with no referent, i.e. simulacrum.

Source: BrendelSignature/CC BY-SA 3.0.

activities of a certain type of family. The exterior has fewer functional determinants and it is here that simulation becomes most evident.[1] Its design is based on projecting an image, evoking an immediate, unreflective response on the part of the viewer. Apart from meeting a few functional demands, making this impression is the design's only intention. Its referents are vague at best. It cannot refer to the values of its owners—how could it when thousands own a nearly identical house? Very few make real historical references and most of these are hopelessly out of context, robbing the reference of its meaning. Subject to cost constraints, its materials are chosen purely for visual effect; otherwise how could people accept a stone veneer that continues barely a foot back from the front façade? We are in Disneyland here, without the markers that set Disneyland apart as a fantasy world.[2]

Most people find these houses perfectly normal, and would bridle at the suggestion that their house belongs in Disneyland. For them, this is what a house is. In part, this is an effect of the housing market. Builders make their products affordable by exploiting economies of scale, and minimize their market risk by building houses similar to those found elsewhere. Buyers need the product and any objections they may have are answered by the fact that everyone they know lives in a similar house. Their preferences thus come to align with what the market produces. Whether people's acceptance of these houses is due to the market, or the market is taking advantage of people's willingness to accept such houses, the result is the same. It does not bother people that these houses are no more than an image thrown over a functional frame, and that the image itself is devoid of any reference except to other, similar houses. They are accustomed to living in a simulation and do not realize that they are.

The same operations that lead people to accept these houses are at work in the built environment at large. There is no need to rehearse the litany of buildings whose exterior design, like that of the houses, does nothing but evoke a vague response. The exterior design of a big-box store *is* that store's sign—the building signifies nothing but the store (Figures 5.3, 5.4, 5.5).[3]

As a mode of reception, simulation thwarts any attempt an architect may make to communicate ideas in their work. A building is not an idea, it can only represent ideas. Absent representation, buildings are simply what they appear to be; the buildings themselves, to echo McLuhan, become the message.

FIGURES 5.3, 5.4, 5.5   The buildings of big-box stores are gigantic signs.

Sources: Figure 5.3 © Stu Pendousmat/CC BY-SA 3.0; Figures 5.4, 5.5 Photo © Brenda Scheer.

Digital Craft

> What all crafts share is not just technique, or hard work on form, but also a probing of their medium's capacity, a passion for practice, and moral value as an activity independent of what is produced.
>
> *(Malcolm McCollough)*[4]

The essence of craftsmanship is the satisfaction of doing good work for its own sake. Where craftsmanship exists, the goal of the work is open-ended. There are no pre-defined criteria for deciding when it is complete. The work is of such a nature that mere adequacy to a task is not enough: something is wanted that exceeds competence and functionality. Craftsmanship is essential to architecture because the work demands deep personal involvement. Simply providing a satisfactory solution to a client's needs is not enough. As the architect defines it, good work requires more. What this "more" is depends on the individual architect, but to be an architect is to believe that this "more" is essential.

Traditional crafts involve working a physical medium with some part of the body, usually the hands. The inherent properties of the medium must be deeply understood by craftsmen. They learn this from long experience with the feedback the medium provides through their tools. The qualities of the medium inform their thinking so that their designs are as much a response to the medium as they are inventions of their imagination. Their work is an encounter with a piece of reality, and this lends it significance. A masterful piece of work testifies to a profound experience of this part of reality. This kind of mastery is not a domination that turns material to its will by force. Rather, it understands the material so intimately that the designer's ideas are expressed without apparent effort; the material helps guide its own working (Figure 5.6). It goes without saying that such craftsmanship is only achieved through long practice, an investment of time and effort that serves to heighten the craftsman's involvement with her work.

Drawing has traditionally been a craft-within-a-craft in architecture that provided aspiring architects with these experiences that bring materiality and the body into architectural design. Mastery of drawing has also been a central part of the architect's professional identity and gaining it was a traditional rite of passage in becoming an architect. Given the decline of drawing, how is architecture to maintain the essential values of craftsmanship?

FIGURE 5.6   The physical qualities of the bamboo determine its curvature, contributing beautifully to the overall form of the basket.

Source: Thamizhpparithi Maari/CC BY-SA 3.0.

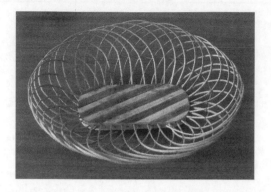

The idea of craftsmanship can be extended to non-material media such as computation. Richard Sennett finds an embodiment of craftsmanship in the community of Linux programmers who donate their time to help develop an operating system for the benefit of the computing community as a whole.[5] Although the medium of computation is non-material, its members are clearly engaged in their work and share the value of doing good work for its own sake. Implicit in traditional craftsmanship is the exploration of the medium, which programmers also do as they search for better ways to accomplish computational tasks.[6] As regards its place in architecture, however, there are two significant differences between the traditional notion of craft and craft as it can be applied to digital work.

One is the lack of a physical connection between maker and materials in computationally-based architecture. Drawing has served architects as a means of learning about the interaction between intention and materials via the body. With digital media, however, this interaction is increasingly mediated by computers, both in design and construction. As this trend continues, the properties of building materials that matter to designers become, not those experienced by a workman, but those that govern a material's workability in CNC machines. The digital designer's tools may not allow him to acquire a bodily understanding of the relationships between material and form, but such an understanding is unnecessary, since the materials are not being worked by humans but by automated machines. Digital fabrication thus changes the relationship of both the designer and the builder to materials. Construction tends to become fabrication (now performed by machines) and the assembly of prefabricated parts (Figure 5.7). In this transition, the body loses much of its importance in the design-construction process.

FIGURE 5.7 Bakoko, The Tahome (2011). This modular house was designed to replace housing destroyed by the 2011 tsunami in Japan. In addition to the usual advantages offered by modular construction, the designers suggest having the units made in the US and then shipped to Japan, which, due to the depressed U.S. economy, would cost less than making them in Japan.

Source: Bakoko/CC BY-ND 2.0.

The second difference is that, whereas the materials of traditional crafts are means of learning about external reality, the digital medium is a human creation. A traditional craftsman absorbs a deep understanding of a part of nature via his mastery of the material he works. The most fundamental lesson he learns is that there is a reality that is independent of his wishes to which he must conform his thinking. In architecture, there is much to be learned about reality by thinking about and working with materials. By their choice of materials and how they are worked, architects express ideas about the world and humanity's place in it (Figure 5.8).

FIGURE 5.8 Alvar Aalto, Villa Mairea, (c. 1938): detail. The design is grounded in the tradition of wood construction in Finland and draws its details from the capacities of that material and the craftsmen who work it.

Source: Frans Drewniak/CC BY 2.0.

Drawing prepares architects to think about materials this way by giving them experience with such choices and allowing them to see how they affect a drawing. By contrast, when a designer encounters the medium of computation, he is not faced with a portion of given reality; he finds an artificial environment where other human beings have written the rules. While computing does have mathematical foundations, a user (the term itself is telling) works with computer languages that ultimately depend on an arbitrary instruction set programmed into a central processing unit by its designers. What can be learned from this encounter only concerns the rules of an artificial language.[7] Architects trained with digital media are less likely to understand design as a response to reality and more likely to see it as creating a world with its own rules, its own reality: in other words, as simulation.

These two differences point in similar directions. Both the immateriality and the artificiality of the computational medium weaken the attachment of architecture to our existential condition as embodied agents in a world that exists outside of ourselves. There are at least two possible responses to this. One is to introduce nature and materiality in simulations. As mentioned in Chapter 4, a great deal of research is being done in immersive and haptic interfaces that engage the body. These are unlikely to succeed in really reproducing real-world experience to a sufficient degree to overcome these problems. Creating a simulation that reproduces all of the aspects of working with a natural material must be extraordinarily detailed. The experience of woodworking, for example, involves not only the response of a tool such as a saw to a species of wood (which varies greatly according to the species and even the particular piece of wood being worked) but also the space and smells of a woodshop, the sounds of tools encountering a piece of material (think of how a table saw screams when it bites into a board) and many other dimensions of experience that all contribute to a woodworker's understanding of his craft. While it is always dangerous to say that something is technologically impossible, the difficulties of creating such a detailed simulation are likely to lead to the acceptance of some degree of simplification and abstraction—an impoverishment of the experience that will not provide a full understanding. In any case, such a simulation lies many years in the future.

The second is to embrace these changes and explore the possibilities of a purely computational craft. Such a practice would take as its central problematic the characteristics of the computational medium described in the previous chapter, exploring, for example, new ideas of order implied by computational geometry and the consequences of design in phase space (Figure 5.9). This would involve empirical as well as com-

FIGURE 5.9   Tanaka Juuyo, *4 Tori* (2013).

Mathematica 8 code for "4 Tori":

```
a = 3; (* center hole size *)
b1 = 5; Zb2 = 2; Zb3 = 5;
c = 3; (* distance from the center of rotation **)
d = 4; (* the number of tori *)
h = 5; (* height of a torus *)

SetOptions[ParametricPlot3D, PlotRange → Full, Mesh → None, Boxed → False,
Axes → False, PlotPoints → 500, ImageSize → 3000, ZBackground →
RGBColor[{200, 200, 240}/255], PlotStyle → Directive[Specularity[White, 90],
Texture[Import["D:/tmp/94.jpg"]]], TextureCoordinateFunction → ({#4/b2, #5 Pi
b1} &), Lighting → "Neutral"];

x = (a − Sin[t] − Sin[b1 s]) Sin[b3 s] + c;
y = (a − Cos[t] − Cos[b1 s]) Cos[b3 s] + c;
z = (a − h Sin[b2 s]) + c;

rm − Table[{x, y, z}.RotationMatrix[2 i Pi/d, {0, 0, 1}], {i, d}];
ParametricPlot3D[rm, {t, 0, 2 Pi}, {s, 0, 2 Pi}]
```

Source: Tanaka Juuyo/CC BY 2.0.

putational research. The artificial genesis of these forms raises questions of the meaning of form in a new context that must dispense with phenomenological notions about its origins in our experience and focus attention on Kantian notions of their basis in the structure of our minds. This kind of architectural investigation would naturally intersect with neuroscience in seeking to shed light on this structure. One also could argue that such an architecture is consistent with simulation as a mode of experience. By struggling to maintain its traditional grounding in the body and reference to an external reality, might architecture doom itself to irrelevance, impotently invoking obsolete values? There are too many unknowns about the possibilities of a purely digital architecture to decide this question out of hand. Both the possibilities for its creation and the modes of its reception need to be explored.

Yet another way to maintain bodily engagement is by means of a hybrid digital–material design process. Such a process pursues material and digital investigations simultaneously and allows them to inform each other. For example, the Terriform project investigated the behavior of sand as a form-finding method to inform both the formal language of the design and the fabrication techniques to construct it.[8] The material research included both the forms that sand naturally assumes on a surface in which openings have been created (Figure 5.10), and a structural system of sand hardened by moistening it with salt water (Figure 5.11). The architects used the information gained from this material research to create computational models to explore the possibilities of building form (Figures 5.12, 5.13, 5.14). There are many other examples of hybrid design practices that employ computational tools together with drawings or physical models such as the 8 Spruce Street project discussed in Chapter 4 (see Figures 4.20, 4.21).[9] To support such a hybrid process, digital models should be displayed in an abstract manner that resists being taken for reality.

The ability of architects to treat computation as a medium depends to a large extent on the nature of their tools, i.e. the software they use. Just as the tools of traditional craftsmen are the means of learning about physical media, so must digital craftsmen have tools that provide knowledge about the computational medium as they work. This is exactly the opposite of the intention behind current software design, which seeks to make the user's experience "transparent" and hide the workings of the software. This causes software designers to make many assumptions about how their products will be used that inevitably turn out to be wrong

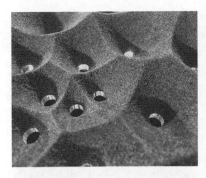

FIGURES 5.10–5.14 35Degree, "Terriform" (2012). The project investigated the behavior of sand as a form-finding method to inform both the formal language of the design and the fabrication techniques to construct it.

Source: © Ahmed Abouelkheir/35Degree.

in a certain number of cases. Such a tool does not help architects learn the qualities of their new medium. In order for computation to achieve the status of a true medium, architects must have tools that provide understanding of it so that they may knowingly turn it to their purposes. Then, perhaps, computational designs will achieve the individuality and authenticity conferred by craft.

Performativity

Performance has always been a value in many aspects of architectural design. Some of architecture's goals can clearly be evaluated objectively: structural stability, reasonable cost, meeting the requirements of a spatial program or a building code, weather-tightness, achieving goals for temperature and humidity, and so on, all admit of objective measurement and evaluation. Other goals cannot be evaluated this way: a building's response to its context, its emotional impact, its relationships to the institution or people it houses and the social interactions it engenders, to name a few. It is generally accepted that architecture has this dual nature, which is unique to it among the arts and frequently an influence on form (Figure 5.15).

FIGURE 5.15   Louis I. Kahn, Richards Medical Research Laboratory (c. 1957). The form of this building was famously shaped by Kahn's notion of servant and served spaces, represented by the towers and blocks respectively.

Given that performative criteria have always applied to architecture to some extent, a critical question has been the balance between these and other ends, which are roughly lumped together here as "expressive." The Vitruvian tradition, perpetuated by Renaissance writers, demanded that architects understand the pragmatic aspects of their art because a poorly-constructed building would damage the architect's reputation.[10] This was only a precondition for architecture; its true fulfillment lay in the realm of art. This schema began to falter in the 19th Century as the technological and economic foundations of the first Industrial Revolution raised effective performance to the status of a universal value. This was reflected in the Modern Movement's efforts to position architecture within the productive system. Le Corbusier advocated the application of engineering design criteria to architecture, a process he called "refinement according to a standard." He saw this as a means of redirecting architects' attention from what he regarded as the empty estheticism of historical styles to the solution of pressing social problems, such as the need for economical mass housing. But he insisted upon the distinction between problem-solving and true architecture. Engineering methods, while they achieve "harmony" and are "on the direct line of good art," are, in his view, insufficient in themselves to create architecture, a "pure creation of the spirit," the purpose of which is to move us. He acutely recognized the dangers to architecture created by the dramatic expansion of the application of performative demands driven by mass society and industrialization. His thinking not only accommodated this expansion, but made of it a positive value that architects could adopt without reducing architecture to the satisfaction of performative criteria.

This was a brilliant strategy for adapting architecture to the increasingly performative values of society while preserving its status as art, but it has proved difficult to put into practice. In architecture, at least, the domains of performance and art cannot be so clearly distinguished. This difficulty, compounded by the vague yet persistent idea that there is more to architecture than pragmatic problem-solving, has kept creative synthesis at the heart of architectural design, a synthesis which forms in the architect's mind. The inaccessibility of this process, often to the architect himself, obliges the formulation and evaluation of design proposals to be based on visible and tangible artifacts of the architect's thinking. To differing degrees, it is understood that the architect's thought process is only partially represented by these artifacts, that there is something going on that eludes precise expression that nevertheless needs to be respected. The mystery of this synthesis, which has been the dike holding performativity back from flooding the plains of architecture, has rested upon the acknowledged gap between physical artifacts and the design itself, in other words, the acceptance of these artifacts as representations of a deeper reality. Simulation dissolves this relationship between artifact and design because it *is* the design, rather than a representation of it. Simulation exhausts the design which may now be evaluated solely on its basis. The moment of synthesis may still have occurred, but the simulation makes no reference to it and does not require it for its understanding.

There is no single "best answer" to architectural design problems. A choice must be made among feasible solutions, striking a balance among the goals of the design. One of the challenges of beginning a design process is to define a "space" of feasible solutions. In traditional design, the architect's experience and judgment were essential for doing this. The time and labor involved in creating design alternatives limited the number that could be considered. Traditional design allows an architect to nurture and explore the possibilities of an idea, often before he is consciously aware of his reasons for pursuing it. His ideas can shift and morph as rapidly as his mind and hand can move. Ideas can remain fluid and mutable for a long time. Simulation-based design tools permit the creation and evaluation of many alternatives, enabling what is called set-based design.[11] Set-based design represents the apotheosis of performativity. Instead of relying on the architect's imagination expressed in a few alternatives, in set-based design, the final design is found from a large number of candidates winnowed according to their performance. Alternatives can be developed to a much higher level of detail before a final selection needs to be made, so that it is based on the greatest possible amount of information.[12] Not only can these tools produce large numbers of trial designs with ease, they automate their evaluation and, in some cases, their selection and further refinement. The speed, ease, and clarity of performative evaluations would leave little room for the consideration of other ideas, even if there was a basis for their discussion. Set-based design is both too slow and too fast. It is too slow to capture fleeting ideas, too fast to allow them to develop in its rush to evaluate them. It puts design ideas under the performative microscope before they have time to mature. Furthermore, knowing that their ideas will be subjected to this process, architects have a great incentive to anticipate the outcome of this performative thinning of the herd and only propose ideas that will be robust under this process. Set-based design thus tends to establish performance as a value in design thinking.

Some writers have tried to save architecture in the newly expanded domain of performativity by taking the word "performance" in its theatrical sense. Buildings are said to perform in this sense because, like a play or a piece of music, they are experienced in time and successive experiences may differ significantly. In the case of buildings, this may be according to the mood and experience of the observer, his familiarity with the building, the conditions of light and weather, and the sensible effects of time on the building.[13] This is a wonderful way to look at buildings, especially as opposed to seeing them as static, independent objects as so many people, even architects, do. Such writings make the very important point that there are other criteria for "performance" than the strictly quantitative, and that, in principle, BIM and computational design are as able to work with these criteria as with the quantitative, technical variety. However, simply choosing to use the word "performance" in this way obscures what is actually at stake. We must not lose sight of the fact that simulation is deeply connected to performativity in the sense used here. Such ideas may provide strategies of resistance to the performative bases of simulation technologies, but the latter must be understood before they can be resisted in a meaningful way.

BIM

The rationale for BIM is almost entirely performative. As previously mentioned, the instigation for its rapid adoption during the last ten years was owners' recognition of the enormous amount of money that drawing errors were costing them.[14] Their original interest in BIM was in avoiding mistakes that dogged drawings, primarily conflicting information and inadequate documentation. The underlying issue was predictability: knowing in advance the cost and duration of a project. BIM improves predictability by simulating construction, which in turn depends on having reliable information about construction methods, cost and schedule. This is information that contractors are best able to provide, leading to the inevitable result that contractors are gaining a role in the design process. This information is most reliable when it is provided by the contractor(s) who will actually be performing the work, and interest has accordingly grown in project delivery methods that permit the contractor to be involved during the design phases of a project. BIM provides predictability in other ways as well. Three-dimensional visualization increases owners' understanding of the project at every stage of design. Using a BIM to verify a design's compliance with its spatial program ensures owners that their building will meet their needs. Simulating various aspects of a building's technical performance, beginning early in the design process, provides owners with information on which to base design decisions, and, as the design matures and these results become more accurate, anticipate some of the costs of operating the building.

Contractors also quickly realized the benefits they stood to gain from BIM. They saw that they could save time and increase their productivity by using BIM to bid and manage projects. Major contractors had the resources and the motivation to implement BIM and to develop innovative uses for it. As a result, large contracting companies are now among the most innovative users of BIM in the industry, outstripping the capabilities of all but the most sophisticated architectural firms. Like owners, contractors are motivated by profit and things like productivity gains and risk reduction are fundamental to their businesses. These two groups are also where a great deal of the industry's resources are found, so it is not surprising that the development of BIM technology has largely served their interests. BIM's original performative impetus has deepened and expanded as the technology has developed.

As has been said, the development of BIM is thus driven, not by architects' needs, but by industry-wide business practices. Business is by nature performative, profit being the overriding metric in most cases. Unfortunately, architects have been along for the ride for the most part. The industry, primarily owners, continues to pressure architects to adopt not only BIM, but the performative values it embodies. Architects' relative reluctance to embrace BIM is not due to a lack of interest in profit, but to the turmoil the transition from drawing to BIM creates in their work and role in the industry. On a psychological level, the deep association between architecture and drawing has been the foundation of architectural culture for so long that it is very difficult for architects trained in this tradition to conceive of architecture any other way. It is part of their identities as architects. On a practical level, architects have a quite accurate sense that their leadership role in building projects is being undermined. As discussed above, drawing places architects at the center of the design process by allowing them to control the flow of information. One important result of this was that the architect was the only member of the design team with a comprehensive overview of the project. BIM gives the entire design team access to this overview; it is no longer the exclusive domain of the architect. The organization of the project team is becoming more horizontal, less a hierarchy than a group of equals. This and the above-mentioned inclusion of the contractor in the design team are consequences of BIM that drastically alter the architect's position in a project. In place of a collection of competing interests, these trends produce a project team whose collective focus is project delivery. As a member of this team, the architect tends to adopt this priority as well.

The old triangular project organization (owner–architect–contractor) has many drawbacks but it does provide the architect with a position from which to advocate design ideas. It implicitly acknowledges the ever-present tension between what is desired and what is possible, which is one of the mainsprings of architectural art. It further creates a natural advocate for each (the architect and the contractor respectively), while obliging both to take the other's point of view into account. Their relationship is often contentious because they bring different values to a project, but the traditional organization provides a framework within which this tension can be productive. By contrast, the members of the integrated team produced by BIM share a common goal: to deliver the project to the owner within the promised price and timeframe or, in some cases, as rapidly and as inexpensively as possible.[15] This reduces conflict, to be sure, but it also diminishes the architect's motivation and ability to be an advocate for design. Put another way, it makes efficient project delivery the architect's primary design value.

To be clear, these are general trends and there are innumerable cases where architects still achieve a substantial degree of design control. The point is that, as these trends become more prevalent, the project structure will not as a matter of course provide a position from which architects can become the authors of the design and the leaders of the project. This role has been under attack for years and BIM will be its final undoing, unless architects find ways of turning the technology to their advantage. Architects can lead, and design ideas can be realized with BIM, but the means of doing this are very different from the traditional setting. Instead of having a ready-made position from which to exercise their authority, architects must now create that position anew with every project. They now need to take seriously the interests and priorities of the other members of the team. Their ideas must be robust in an intensely collaborative, performative environment. They must learn how to use the analytical power of BIM to justify their proposals, for example, by showing that an idea that seems impractical at first glance is actually not only feasible but advantageous. Or, they may be able to establish a consensus at the outset around certain ideas that will drive the design, making them, in effect, performance criteria. But the greatest challenge for architects is to avoid accepting performance as their own principal design value. We have seen that BIM, and simulation in general, embody performativity. In order to maintain other values, architects need to place BIM in a context that allows them to see it, not as the project in virtual form, but as one of many ways of describing it; to see it, in other words, as a representation.

Computational Design

Computational design has its roots in the explorations of systems theory by architects in the 1960s. This movement, which included such architects as Christopher Alexander, Nicholas Negroponte, and Gordon Pask, sought to design buildings as holistic systems whose properties emerge from the interactions among their parts.[16] They subscribed to a computerized version of the Corbusian idea that a design solution should emerge from the demands of the design problem itself, and hoped that computers would allow a larger number of more complex criteria to be taken into consideration. Gradually, most of them realized that this required a degree of abstraction that caused design problems to lose their true architectural character.[17] This problem turned out largely to be a function of the technical and conceptual limitations of computation at that time. Current forms of computational design can take advantage of much more powerful computers and are based on more sophisticated computational techniques. These do not try to impose a preconceived idea of the holistic behavior of the design as systems theory did, but allow this behavior to emerge, along with the form, from the design constraints themselves.

The complexity of design problems as formulated by computational design prevents a performative definition of design in the sense of BIM. Allowing many practical constraints and requirements to work themselves out instead of trying to imagine solutions upfront gives results that are literally unimaginable. Recursive algorithmic processes end up being non-deterministic in spite of the determinism of the individual algorithms (Figure 4.19). The complexity of the interactions among various conditions, iterated many times, can produce emergent order that is impossible to foresee. Slight variations in the initial conditions provided by the designer to start the process can lead to dramatically different results. If performativity imposes clear, objective criteria for design decisions, this does not fit the description.

Performance criteria are a formal requirement in computational design processes. They play an essential role in selecting certain members of a population to become the basis for succeeding populations (Figure 4.15). But the nature of the criteria is open as long as they fulfill this role. With this proviso, any characteristic the architect may want his design to have can be termed "performance" for purposes of computational design. They need not pertain to building performance as usually understood.

An example of this is 8 Spruce Street by Gehry Partners, discussed in Chapter 4 (Figures 4.20, 4.21). Here a primary criterion is adherence to a design idea. To be a candidate for further development, a solution had to display a sufficient degree of formal resemblance to the physical model that embodied the design intention. Although this criterion was not related to the building's performance in the usual sense, the designers found a way to express it parametrically that allowed the computer to apply it to the forms it generated. In this way, the role of computational design in the overall design process was that of a tool in service of an expressive idea. Somewhat paradoxically, expression becomes a performative criterion.

Another example is the finding of so-called "minimal surfaces." A soap bubble is an example of a minimal surface: the surface tension in

FIGURE 5.16 Frei Otto, Cologne Dance Fountain, Open Air Stage (c. 1957). Tensile structures like these use materials in tension as a form-finding system.

Source: Raimond Spekking/CC BY-SA 3.0.

FIGURE 5.17 Shajay Bhooshan et al., "Learning from Candela" (2012). This form was found by setting boundary curves and minimizing the curvature of the surface connecting them. The process is far from automatic, however. The designers had to intervene at many points to create a working system that met site and constructional constraints.

Source: © Shajay Bhooshan, et al.

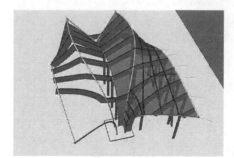

FIGURE 5.18 The computational model shows the boundary curves and the two-dimensional plane of the minimal surface that generate the form. These had to be modified to accommodate fabrication and construction.

Source: © Shajay Bhooshan, et al.

FIGURE 5.19 The boundary curves are set by the curved tubes visible in this photograph. Due to constraints of fabrication, each of these had to lie in a single plane.

Source: © Shajay Bhooshan, et al.

FIGURE 5.20   The placement of the rebar was constrained by the boundary tubes and offset from the wooden frames.

Source: © Shajay Bhooshan, et al.

FIGURE 5.21   The shell is created by manually applying concrete over the rebar mesh. It required craftsmanship to achieve a smooth finished surface. This aspect of computational design is often cited by its practitioners as highly satisfying, but it is not an inherent part of the design fabrication process. In fact, the properties of the concrete shell were not used in the computational model to find the final form, which is actually based on a draped fabric (Bhooshan, 2013).

Source: © Shajay Bhooshan, et al.

the soap film is minimized by its spherical shape. This "analog" form-finding is also demonstrated by the tensile structures of Frei Otto (Figure 5.16). The "Learning from Candela" project in Mexico City is an example of computational form-finding (Figures 5.17, 5.18, 5.19). In this example, the form's boundaries were set and a surface of minimal curvature was found computationally meeting these boundaries (Figures 5.20, 5.21).[18] The criterion of minimal curvature is not related to building performance,[19] yet it serves the formal purpose of a performance criterion for the form-finding process. As a further distancing from performativity, the choice of the boundaries was made by the designers, limited by the need, imposed by the computational process, for these to lie in a plane. There were also other parameters the designers needed to provide before the problem could be solved successfully.[20] This form, like all forms found in similar fashion, is thus not determined by performative processes alone. This is another way computational design can evade strict performativity. As this example demonstrates, these processes involve the designer's direct intervention at several points. In the opinion of most theorists and practitioners of computational design, its purpose is not to automate design, but rather to suggest possibilities that would not otherwise have occurred to the designer.[21] The designer can "stir the pot" at any time, either by directly selecting certain candidates or by modifying the algorithmic structure of the model. As in any design process, the designer may or may not be aware of his reasons for making such decisions. There are two conditions created by computational design that make such intuitive decisions more difficult to incorporate. The first is that they appear to conflict with a premise of the process, to wit, that its solutions are valid because they emerge from the problem. Admitting intuition as a valid basis for decisions vitiates this claim. Computational design is caught in a bind: while seeking to base form on the conditions acting upon that form, it also recognizes the need for the designer to affect form, both to make needed design decisions that the conditions themselves do not motivate, and to allow expression. What are lacking are criteria for making these unmotivated decisions which at present seem to be guided by the subjective visual appeal of the final result.

The second condition is more difficult. Intuitive interventions in the computational process could be welcomed as they are in traditional design, if we knew how to assess the final outcome. However a designed object is created, tradition can assume that whatever effects an object has on its viewers are the intelligible result of the designer's intentions (whether or not he himself is aware of them). The designer's intentions in these works are mediated by processes whose effects the designer cannot anticipate. Interpreting them as the expression of the designer's intention misses half the point, which is precisely the use of methods that are not totally under the designer's control, that introduce essential components of the design in ways he cannot completely comprehend. An analogous situation exists on the part of the viewer whose experience may likewise be the product of digital media. New modes of reception need to be discovered to allow computationally designed objects to be appreciated on their own terms. This can be seen in the responses of even sophisticated critics to such objects. Here is *New York Times* architecture critic Michael Kimmelman on the Barclays Center in Brooklyn (Figure 5.22):

> The arena opened around a month ago, a hunkered-down, hunch-backed, brooding sight at the intersection of Flatbush and Atlantic Avenues. At first blush it's a shocker, which is one of its virtues. Its rusted, reddish-brown exterior consists of 12,000 grainy weathered-steel panels, each one a little different, devised by the latest computer modeling: a digital-age extrusion of hard-core industrial

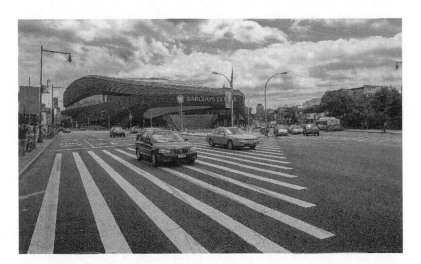

FIGURE 5.22   SHoP Architects, Barclays Center (c. 2012). View from street.

Source: © David Kutz.

glamor . . . The architects have created something tougher, more textured and compelling, an anti-Manhattan monument, not clad in glass or titanium but muscular and progressive like its borough.[22]

Kimmelman vividly describes his impressions but hardly dares to interpret them. He values the building's novelty ("a shocker") and what it is not (Manhattan), but he appears unable to say what it *is* or what it might mean.

Conclusion

Architecture presently is split between representation and simulation. Representation persists thanks to long tradition and the continuing activity of a large number of practicing architects trained to think with drawing. Nevertheless, the outlines of architecture and building in the domain of simulation are becoming clear. BIM is facilitating architecture's complete assimilation into the building production process and forcing it to embrace the latter's performative logic. This logic either deprives architecture's expressive ambitions of legitimacy or remakes them in its own image. Simulation dispenses with any relationship to materials and the haptic knowledge of the external world they provide. The craftsmanship so essential for the architect's involvement with her work loses its material basis. The public, which by and large experiences their environment as simulation, rewards works that satisfy its craving for stimulation. On the other hand, in possible compensation, the medium of computation is offered to architects as a kind of second nature for their exploration and a partner that extends their cognitive capacities, introducing a fascinating if (because?) alien element into design.

It is pointless to mourn these developments. Individual architects can retain the old values and practices if they like, but the discipline as a whole is already engaged in a radically different world. The conditions for architecture created by simulation seem barren in the light of traditional ideas, but may present new possibilities if seen through different eyes. To continue as architects, we must change our ideas.

Notes

1 Not that the interiors are any less simulation. "Typical patterns of the daily activities" is a simulacrum that displaces actual life as lived by a fictitious construct that actually describes no one's life. Likewise, "a certain type of family" is a fiction that displaces real families. The real people who eventually inhabit these houses and the real lives they lead are cast in the mold of these simulacra. Attempts to reclaim the house for real life (e.g. decorating and customizing) are usually futile. These simulacra are deeply embedded in its basic planning which is difficult and expensive to alter. Families generally have no choice but to live in this simulation.

2 These markers hide the fact that our "real" world is no more real than Disneyland. As Baudrillard writes: "Disneyland is presented as imaginary in order to make us believe that the rest is real . . ." (Baudrillard, 1994, p. 12).

3 What the store signifies as a place to shop is another story: a carefully crafted brand whose precision and sophistication are the opposite of the muteness of the design and routine construction of the building. A young person whose goal is to design environments could do worse than to become a brand manager at a marketing firm.

4 McCullough (1998, p. 29).

5 Sennett (2008, p. 24 ff.).

6 McCullough (1998, p. 29).

7 Early text-based computer games such as "The Wizard's Cave" could be seen as metaphors for computing itself. Playing the game involved discovering the rules its creators had established which required solving logical puzzles and finding hidden patterns—the same skills programming requires.

8 Abouelkheir, Shahi, Lee, & Wong (2012).

9 For additional examples, see Heumann (2012).

10 According to Alberti:

> A well-constructed building will enhance the renown of anyone who has invested understanding, attention, and enthusiasm in the matter, yet equally, should the wisdom of the designer or the competence of the workman be found wanting, it will greatly detract from his reputation and good name.
>
> (1988, p. 33)

11 Singer, Doerry, & Buckley (2009).

12 Deutsch (2011).

13 See, for example, Leatherbarrow (2005) and Kolarevic (2005).

14 Construction Users Roundtable (2004).

15 This is the case with true Integrated Project Delivery (IPD) in which the entire design/construction team stands to receive a bonus if the project is completed ahead of schedule or under budget.

16 Christopher Alexander summarized the goals of this movement as follows:

> [T]o ensure the holistic system properties of buildings and cities, we must invent generating systems whose parts and rules will create the necessary holistic system properties of their own accord . . . This is a radical step in the conception of design. Most designers today think of themselves as designers of objects . . . The designer becomes a designer of generating systems—each capable of generating many objects—rather than a designer of individual objects.
>
> (2011, p. 66)

17 Alexander also states:

> The discipline of abstraction has one drawback. Occasionally we are confronted with phenomena which are clearly the products of interactions— but the interactions are so complex that we cannot see them clearly, and we cannot make the effort of abstraction successfully.
>
> (2011, p. 62)

18 Bhooshan (2013).
19 Minimal curvature could be a performative requirement if minimizing the surface area of the structure were desired. In this example, at least, the designers used it as a criterion in form-finding, not because they wanted to minimize the surface area (Bhooshan, 2013).
20 Bhooshan (2013).
21 Kostas Terzides expresses this idea as follows: "The power of computation, which involves vast quantities of calculations, combinatorial analysis, randomness, or recursion, to name a few, point out [sic] to new 'thought' processes that may have not ever occurred to the human mind" (Terzides, 2006, p. 18).
22 Kimmelman (2012).

6
SIMULATION AND IDEATION

Introduction

The changes caused by BIM and computational design go deeper than their effects on architects' working methods. Building design and production are being integrated into the performative structure of the general economy to a greater degree than ever before. The barriers that once shielded architecture to some extent from this stringent performative pressure were largely due to the inherent inefficiencies of drawing as its chief medium of communication. As these tools replace drawing for performative economic reasons, they challenge the ideational underpinnings of an architecture based on drawing and the organization of design and construction it created and perpetuated.

Intimately related to this process is the pervasive cultural phenomenon of simulation in which experience is perceived without reference and origins, reduced to its immediate effects, its operational equivalent, that can be evaluated by performative criteria. The popular reception of the built environment has been conditioned by simulation for a half century or more, but architects have for the most part ignored this, retaining an understanding of their discipline as capable of communicating ideas and participating in a public discourse. This understanding of architecture relied upon drawing which trained architects to think in terms of representation. The shift to design tools that are based on simulation deprives architects of the support drawing provided for this representational understanding of architecture and the world in general.

Our focus throughout the book has been on general effects of the encroachment of simulation on architecture. Such generalizations are dangerous, so a couple of caveats might be in order. First, in examining simulation's effects on architecture and construction, the reader should bear in mind that, under the present circumstances, it is impossible to make valid generalizations about "*the* construction industry" or "*the* practice of architecture." The industry as a whole and architectural practice in particular are far from uniform. Great disparities exist in how projects are designed and built depending on their scale, the capabilities of their designers and builders, and the demands of their owners. These disparities are exacerbated by varying degrees of adoption of the technologies under discussion. Because the latter are developing rapidly, the industry must continually invest in new software and in learning how best to use it. Because the technologies are relatively new, many owners are still unsure how to realize the advantages they provide, and many project teams lack experience in implementing them effectively. The largest gap is along the lines of project size. Due to their greater logistical challenges and the sheer amount of money involved, larger projects stand to gain the greatest benefits from technology-enabled processes. These projects generally employ larger design and contracting firms whose greater resources and project volume allow them to develop such processes in ever-more sophisticated ways.

Second, the observations in this book regarding performativity apply most directly to architectural practices competing in the general market for design services and rigorously subject to its demands. As we know, there are special practices whose reputation attracts clients who place greater value on design than on market responsiveness. While such practices are not immune to the pressures of performance and cost, their special status gives them greater latitude and resources to explore novel ideas than is given the typical firm. The work of these practices tends to attract more notice both from the general public and architects themselves. The expectations of both groups are thereby formed by projects that are possible only under special circumstances, a fact that generally goes unremarked-upon. On the other hand, these special cases are important both because the projects created by these architects can extend the perceived boundaries of the possible, and because they perpetuate the idea of the architect as the creative mind behind building. Other architects can benefit by studying these innovative projects and applying the ideas they find in them to their own work. They can also use these projects as case studies to demonstrate the feasibility of certain ideas and the validity of innovative thinking in general. Furthermore, their collaborators may be more inclined to grant them greater design authority by the image of the architect sustained by these signature projects. Nevertheless, it is misleading to judge the general state of architecture by the work of these firms. They are created under conditions that differ in important ways from those that prevail on the vast majority of projects. In particular, this obscures the increasing predominance of performance criteria.

Finally, simulation is both responsible for and reinforced by BIM and computational design. These tools evolved to address performance-driven building problems, which continue to shape their development and use. However, they do not need to be used exclusively in this way. BIM and computational design are techniques that can be applied in many ways and developed in many different directions. If architecture wishes to avoid becoming instrumentalized, the challenge is to intervene in the cycle in which (a) the understanding of building as solving performative problems drives (b) the development of tools which (c) cause buildings to be understood as performative objects.

Receptive Competence

For architecture to represent, its public needs to regard buildings as things that require and sustain interpretation. This is not a conscious attitude but a mode of perception that sees the world as composed of signs. Understood in this way, architecture can play a role in public discourse. Beyond any individual, hermetic experience of a building, the interplay of its architectural signifiers and socio-cultural signifieds can be analyzed and discussed publicly: how architecture represents ideas, the values that are implicit in a particular representation of an institution, the nature of a particular activity and similar issues are raised by architecture as questions for public discussion. What is at stake in the displacement of representation by simulation is not architecture's ability to move people, but its status as public discourse.

With simulation, the world is not seen as composed of signs. Reference to any external reality is absent; the world is reduced to its operational aspects, i.e., its perceptible effects on the senses. In this mode, people do not seek to interpret their surroundings; they are immersed in their experience. The initial moment of the encounter with a work of architecture, its immediate emotional impact and the spontaneous upwelling of personal memories and associations: all this remains. But this is also where the interaction with the work stops. Giotto's campanile in Venice is the place where you met your friend ten years ago and brings back memories of that day. It is also an image that you associate with Venice. These things become the significance of a work of architecture in the mode of simulation.

The vast bulk of our society now experiences the built environment as simulation. Evidence for this is in the built environment itself: the ubiquity of superficial architectural "environments" (Figure 6.1), the nearly universal preference for pseudo-historical motifs in newly-designed public places (Figure 6.2), the embrace of explicitly simulated environments for everyday activities (Figures 6.3, 6.4), and so on. This is being extended and intensified by simulation technologies that are increasingly interposed between people and the built environment. These are both incorporated into the environment itself and carried or worn by people.[1]

FIGURE 6.1 The popularity of "environments" like this indicates a general lack of public interest in meaningful reference in their surroundings.

Source: Photo © Brenda Scheer.

FIGURE 6.2 A new mid-block street in San Luis Obispo. Diluted, ersatz historicism. Pure image: simulation.

Source: Photo © Brenda Scheer.

FIGURE 6.3 The Borgata shopping mall in Scottsdale, AZ, was built in 1981 as a "replica" of the famous Tuscan hill town of San Gimignano. It became a landmark for local residents who have recently mounted an effort to preserve it from plans to redevelop the site for residential use.

Source: Photo by Dru Bloomfield.

FIGURE 6.4 A tower at the Borgata—the key element in the referenced image of San Gimignano. Note the careful framing in both photographs emphasizing the picturesque appeal of the architecture.

Source: Photo by Terry Ballard.

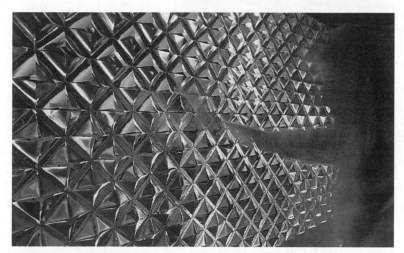

FIGURE 6.5 Studio Roosegaarde, *Lotus 7.0* (2010). An example of interactive architecture created using computational design. "'Lotus 7.0' is a living wall made out of smart foils which fold open in response to human behavior. Walking by 'Lotus 7.0', hundreds of aluminium foils unfold themselves organically; generating transparent voids between private and public" (from the architect's website).

Source: Studio Roosegaarde.

The former category includes architectural-scale digital displays that transform static walls into animated surfaces, often changing in response to the presence and activity of people nearby (Figure 6.5). Environmental installations that change their spatial configuration are also becoming more common as well as an interest in architectural spaces that respond dynamically to their inhabitants (Figure 6.6). In the domain of technologies carried on the body, the near-universal use of smartphones alters the experience of the built environment profoundly. Through

FIGURE 6.6 Philip Beesley, *Sargasso* (2011). An interactive installation that changes its form in response to the proximity and movement of people.

Source: © Philip Beesley.

these devices, individuals craft their own experience of which the physical built environment is only one component and a background one at that. As their bodies move through one space, they are likely to be engaged visually and aurally with people and activities taking place elsewhere or nowhere: text messages, phone calls, social media, websites, photographs, videos, personal and multi-player games, and on and on. If architecture concerns the shaping of spatial experience, these technologies must be regarded as having architectural effects. The melding of such disparate forms of experience into a coherent whole can only take place under the sign of simulation where causes are ignored and experience itself becomes the message. Electronically and physically generated experiences are compatible because their disparate origins are of no consequence in the domain of simulation.

In this connection, augmented reality deserves special mention (Figure 6.7). As its name implies, the intent of this technology is to produce a new type of experience, not simply to add to the existing one (otherwise it would be called "annotated reality"). In this it is similar to signage which

FIGURE 6.7 An historical view of this London street is superimposed on the actual street by an augmented reality app. The design possibilities of augmented reality are vast.

Source: Image by Alan Levine.

becomes part of a streetscape. Its text, graphics, and hyperlinks could not become part of the environment were it not for the conditions that simulation creates that detach experience from cause and allow different kinds of stimuli to coexist on an equal footing. As this technology becomes ubiquitous, environments will be designed based on its effects. It will become impossible to interpret one's surroundings without it. At that point, the human subject alone is inadequate; technological enhancement is essential and we can again speak of a hybrid subject whose experience is created and interpreted by an inseparable entity composed of human being and computer.

The most significant effects of the displacement of representation by simulation on architecture are focused in a few key areas which will now be discussed.

Intentionality and Authorship

In order to find ideas in a building, people first have to believe that something is being communicated with them through it. In order for there to be a message there has to be a sender. The dyad of sender and receiver is fundamental to the act of interpretation; otherwise there could be no communication, nothing for the receiver to receive. Moreover, the receiver needs to believe that the various messages communicated by a building are parts of a coherent whole. This is needed for the interpretation of the messages, since individually these are usually ambiguous. The whole becomes the context that allows the interpretation of the parts and vice versa. The coherent whole is the architect's intention—the ideas they intended to convey. Interpreting a building involves discerning the architect's intentions. The architect thus becomes one of the building's signifieds, present as the author of the intentions it manifests and thus the guarantor of the building's intelligibility. It is largely on this basis that the architect is considered the author of the building.

A necessary ingredient of architects' claim to authorship is their ability to use a building project to express their intentions, as opposed to expressing the intentions of someone else or none at all. As a result of the Renaissance assertion of rationality, the principles of design became the type of knowledge proper to the architect, a quasi-autonomous discourse that set the framework within which both architects and society at large understood architecture. This provided the basis for the architect's claim to authority over, and thereby authorship of, a project. The real architecture resided in the architect's ideas, and buildings acquired cultural significance as embodiments of these ideas. As direct expressions of the architect's thought, drawings could be considered closer to architecture than the building they described. This has led Mario Carpo to propose that buildings created under this paradigm were ideally direct transcriptions of the architect's drawings.[2] This priority of ideas over building still sustains most architectural education and shapes architects' design thinking, even in the face of changing social and cultural realities.

These bases of the architect's authorship of a building are demolished by simulation. First, the notion of intention is displaced by a transformation of the nature of the architect as designing subject. One aspect of this arises from the increasing necessity for computation in design. Computers are effectively extending human cognitive capacities. BIM's ability to store and process such vast quantities of data allows architects and other designers to bring an immense amount of information to bear on their work. The radically expanded capacity of a BIM-enabled architect to make effective use of information redefines the design task in ways we have seen, enabling analysis to guide design to a previously unimaginable extent and permitting the design and execution of qualitatively more complex projects. As regards computational design, the forms it generates are the products of processes of which humans are incapable. Computational design provides architects with entirely new ways of thinking about form, generating them from sets of relationships and constraints rather than visualizing them directly. The cognitive enhancements computers provide designers are of a qualitative rather than a quantitative nature. They do not merely perform tasks faster; they perform tasks that humans alone cannot perform at all. A design process based on these enhancements contains characteristics of two radically different ways of processing information and is therefore best understood as the product of a hybrid human-computer subject. The cognitive capabilities of this subject are neither those of a human nor those of a computer, but of a third, genuinely new, type of entity.

Whereas computational design creates a hybrid design subject, computationally-enabled collaboration creates a collective one. The design team emerges as the relevant cognitive entity behind a building design. The performative logic of BIM tends to unify the motivations of team members to make project delivery as efficient as possible. This is an

intention of sorts, but the only one such a process can convey. It is interesting to note that human-computer interaction (HCI) research has
developed models of so-called distributed cognition, i.e., people pos-
sessing various types of knowledge functioning as a single cognitive
unit.[3] Based on these models, these researchers are designing software to
support decision-making by such a collective subject,[4] as well as new
interfaces that will incorporate other senses in addition to the visual and
enhance interactivity such as those discussed in Chapter 5.[5] This research
should interest architects and the companies that design the software
they use.

This leads to the second source of traditional authorship eliminated by
simulation: architects' ability to express their intentions in their projects.
As we have seen, an architect in a BIM-based collaborative design team
is far from certain to be in a position to do this. The position of the architect within such teams varies on each project, according to the dynamic
that is established within each design team. The uncertainty of the architect's position is due to a shift in the nature of the knowledge architects
are supposed to have. Universal principles of architectural design,
such as were believed to exist by Renaissance culture, are no longer
regarded as true knowledge. They have been replaced by notions of
personal style or taste, about which, as everyone knows, no discussion is
possible. Nevertheless, architects manage to preserve some authority on
this basis, while acquiring other important skills: information management, coordination of design teams, and the ability to grasp a project
comprehensively. With the advent of BIM, these skills are no longer the
exclusive province of architects. The technology performs these functions
to a large extent and, with shared information, everyone can have a
comprehensive view of the project. Still, someone has to do it, and that
is a large part of the architect's job. But the most important part of
the architect's job is originating the design of the building. Although the
architect's autonomy has been restricted by the dominance of performative design criteria, this is still something only architects can do. The
architect's ability to express intentions through the project rests largely
on the strength of these initial ideas. These ideas are now subject to rapid
performative judgment, a new condition architects will have to learn to
contend with. However, architects can still lead by virtue of their ideas,
and design, as traditionally understood, must remain the heart of the
architect's training.

Both these transformations of the designing subject require a rethinking of the nature of design ideas. They relocate design thinking from the individual mind to either a hybrid with different cognitive characteristics, or to a collective in which cognition is distributed. In either case, the nature of an idea that is appropriate for guiding a design process is transformed. In the first case, such an idea must directly be conceived as a set of relationships, not an object. It must be expressed in computer code which has its own rules and structure which influence how an idea may be expressed. In the second case, it must be based on (or argued for in terms of) performative values in order to be accepted by the designing collective.

Function and Expression

The traditional architectural design problem has a dual nature, having both functional and expressive aspects. The Vitruvian formula of *Firmitas, Commoditas, Venustas* (Firmness, Commodity, Delight) summarized the problem succinctly: buildings should be solidly constructed, appropriately house the people, activities and institutions within and provide esthetic pleasure for their inhabitants and beholders. Reconciling or balancing these three goals of architecture was a touchstone of architectural theory until the second half of the 20th Century. The dynamism of the dialectic between need (function) and expression (form) drives much of traditional architecture. For some architects, the pursuit of this dynamic is the distinguishing trait of architecture as opposed to mere building.[6]

With simulation, architectural expression, like everything else, is defined operationally. It is evaluated solely on the basis of its observable effects, in this case the human responses it induces. This is precisely how many environments are designed today, with performative goals of inducing behavior such as shopping which can be objectively measured by sales (Figure 6.8). In this case, the architect again has a unique type of knowledge: how to design environments that induce desired patterns of behavior. Most architects today do not accept such environments as serious architecture, yet these are the places our society often chooses to build for itself. This is where simulation leads unless something deters it.

For the time being, at least, most architects and a substantial portion of the public still want architecture to be expressive and not entirely

FIGURE 6.8

A modern shopping mall environment calculated to generate sales.

Source: Photo © Brenda Scheer.

functional. Any expression, however, must be accomplished within the larger regime of performativity which governs the general conditions under which buildings are built. Expressive concerns are at a disadvantage with respect to functional considerations because the latter lend themselves to performative evaluation much more naturally. Yet there are ways of reconciling expression with the performative domain. One is to exempt expression from performative evaluation. In a society whose values are performative, this denies expression grounds for legitimacy and excludes it from public discourse, exposing it to the risk of empty expressionism. Another is to limit expression to portions of the design not determined by expressly performative criteria. The pattern of mullions in a curtain wall once the structural loads have been accommodated would be one such opportunity. Both of these approaches subordinate expression to performance and eliminate it from the core purpose of architecture which remains strictly performative. A more interesting approach is to install expressive ideas at the outset of the project so that they become, in effect, performative criteria for the remainder of the design. This is

FIGURES 6.9 AND 6.10 Studio Gang, Solar Carve project (ongoing). The form of the building envelope was designed computationally to allow as much sunlight as possible to fall on the High Line Park adjacent to the site.

Source: Images © Studio Gang Architects.

the strategy employed by Gehry Partners in the 8 Spruce Street project (Figure 4.20). While this approach allows greater expressive freedom than the first two, the means of achieving the proposed expressive goals are subject to performance testing and cost analysis (a species of performance) before they can be adopted (Figure 4.21). Only certain owners are willing to support such a process and trust the architect that the exploration will result in a feasible design.

Yet another approach is offered by computational design: to use the project's performance criteria to find a form. An example of this is the Solar Carve project by Studio Gang Architects. The form is shaped by the performative goal of minimizing the shadow it casts on the adjacent High Line Park (Figures 6.9, 6.10). This example also overcomes the problem of communicating intention with simulation. The choice of the performative goal expresses the value that the architects set on public space. Unlike many computational design projects, however, the architects of this project did not allow the computational process to obscure their intentions. This was possible because the shading criterion affects the form directly and apparently did not conflict with any other criteria.

The Body

The body plays a critical if often unacknowledged role in traditional architectural design. We do not experience space as a pair of disembodied eyes, but though all of our senses, including our kinesthetic sense that responds to our bodies' movement. Although this fact of our experience is rarely mentioned in architectural theory (outside of phenomenology[7]), every good architect is acutely aware of its effects on the experience of buildings (Figures 6.11, 6.12). Somewhat paradoxically, drawing incorporates such spatial experience into design through the immense abstraction of reducing spatial experience to two-dimensional, linear geometric constructions. This abstraction is the key to drawing's use as a design tool. With experience, architects learn to imaginatively inhabit the spaces they are designing, transmuting a shape on a sheet of paper into a tangible space surrounding their bodies. The very abstraction of drawing begs for this inhabitation in order to get beyond graphic impressions (what Le Corbusier called "the illusion of plans") to the experience of the space.

FIGURE 6.11 Lichfield Cathedral, interior. The scale, proportions and lighting create a sense of awe and otherworldliness.

Source: Photo by Michael D. Beckwith.

FIGURE 6.12 Frank Lloyd Wright, Price Tower, interior (c. 1956). The low ceilings, shadows and warm materials create a sense of intimacy.

Source: Photo © Brenda Scheer.

The body is also central to the traditional architectural understanding of materials. The connections among material properties, craftsmanship, drawing, and architecture have been discussed. The tactile experience of drawing materials gives architects an experience of the reciprocity of thought and its material expression which is also present in construction. Drawing also added a tactile, hence bodily, dimension to the act of design, describing a form with the hand as it left its visible trace on paper. The body has also had a profound influence on architectural design where one might not think to look for it: in the geometry that underlies traditional building design.

Current architectural simulation interfaces provide very little bodily engagement, but this limitation will be overcome in due course. This will be a great improvement and will restore the body to design in ways that may mimic drawing or engage the body more fully. The possibilities of new interfaces should certainly be explored and will lead to entirely new relationships among the act of designing, design thinking, and building that are difficult to imagine now. Differences will remain, however, between a simulation, however realistic, and real bodily experience. Simulations are operational: they give only experience, not its causes. At some point, further investigation of experience in a simulation yields only information about the simulation itself. Simulations are programmed: everything that happens in them is foreseen in some way. They can contain programmed irregularities but not actual accidents. But more important than the qualities of the interface is the mode of perception. The essence of simulation is operationalism that allows the identity of model and building. This is what produces performativity and all that it entails for architecture.

Geometry

Geometry's influence on traditional architectural thought appears in two distinct yet interrelated domains: the relationship between thought and design and that between physical buildings and our experience of them. In both cases the dual nature of geometric forms as both ideal (perceived by our minds) and material (drawn or built, perceived by our embodied senses) allows architecture to mediate these two otherwise disparate domains. In this way, it is an essential medium for architectural representation.

The concrete uses of geometry in the design and building process itself are signs of deeper influences of geometry on architectural thought. What might be called the pragmatics of geometry results from the projective nature of the relationships between our thought and our imagination, between imagination and drawing, between drawings and buildings, and between our perceptual experience and the buildings themselves.[8] In modeling these relationships on projection, we create a formal analogy among the three processes of the formation of mental images from ideas, the genesis of drawings from mental images and the construction of buildings from drawings. The operation of projection made of drawing the intermediate term between the ideal world and the physical.

As pointed out in Chapter 4, simulation employs virtual rather than physical objects. This not only disrupts the multi-level analogy described above, it also deprives the designer of ambiguity, forcing precise description at inappropriate stages of the design's development. Any object of virtual geometry has an inhuman precision. A computer calculates the location of every point in a figure to many decimal places; one cannot tell it "Put it somewhere around here." Eventually a building design must commit to precise locations for each of its points, but during the design process excessive accuracy can be misleading and may prematurely foreclose design possibilities. Equivocation not only can be productive, it is sometimes essential. Drawing is often purposely—and productively—vague. Furthermore, it permits movement among different representations of an idea without requiring that these have a definite relationship to each other or to the object—or that the object itself be well-defined (Figure 6.13). An architect need not commit to an undeveloped aspect of the design in order to explore others. The computer, on the other hand, demands exactitude. The first computerized "sketch" of a design has the same degree of precision as the final version. In spite of its actual uncertainty, the precision of a preliminary computer model lends it an aura of finality that tends to discourage change and experimentation at the moment when they are most needed. This is all to say that computational geometry does not perform the same epistemological functions as drawing. One can speak about exploration with a computer in the sense that one can try many possibilities, but each of these must be precisely described. This is very different from exploration by means of drawing, where nothing need be precise, allowing rapid and wide-ranging movement among ideas.

FIGURE 6.13 John Hejduk, *House of Farm Community Master Builder* (1982–83). In this drawing, the architect explores three-dimensional and two-dimensional form, construction details, formal (and material?) ideas such as a guitar, and verbal descriptions of its inhabitant. He moves quickly among these various modes and builds up a multi-dimensional notation that combines spatial and discursive ideas. Finalizing a form is clearly not his goal, but understanding what the relationships among form, material and activity may be.

Source: John Hejduk, fonds Collection Centre Canadien d'Architecture/Canadian Centre for Architecture, Montréal.

A remarkable property of virtual geometry is that the human mind perceives many of its products an form, that is, having a perceptible underlying order, rather than an arbitrary shape. The fascinating conclusion is that the mind can recognize geometric patterns that apparently do not arise from our experience. For example, Husserl's account of ideal geometric forms was that they are "limit shapes" we intuit based on the empirical shapes we encounter in our experience. We see many things that are roughly circular, for example, and extrapolate from them the *idea* of circularity.[9] The forms that arise in computational geometry clearly have a different origin and discovering what that might be is a fertile field for architectural research that may shed light on our understanding of space and form.

Object, Set and Population

The traditional design process focuses on a single design. At the outset, many ideas are explored in sketches, but one design soon emerges that becomes the final project. The development process could be described as an effort to perfect the design. It is understood that perfection will never be attained, but nevertheless there is an ideal the architect strives to achieve. In the process, the architect becomes committed to the design, which is carefully studied and its possibilities thoroughly explored. In different ways, BIM and computational design abandon this commitment.

BIM enables set-based design, a process wherein many alternatives are quickly generated, analyzed, and sorted. The speed of the computer allows this to be done quickly so that many ideas can be tested. The process also depends on the BIM's capacity to store a great deal of data about a design in spite of a low level of spatial development. Using this data and the simple geometry of the model, the performance of several parameters of the design can be determined, such as construction cost, energy performance relative to other alternatives and HVAC requirements. The structural frame can be quickly designed and materials assigned to each model element to allow the cost estimate to be based on quantity take-offs rather than the less accurate cost-per-square-foot basis. The designers can study the massing of the building on its site, verify that it meets codes and program area and consider site development. In short, a great deal of analysis can be done very quickly, based on a very simple BIM. The speed with which these analyses can be performed also makes it economical to further develop several alternatives to a fairly high level, making the analyses more accurate. The commitment to a final design can take place fairly late in the process when its characteristics are well understood. Best performance replaces the traditional ideal goal of design.

As described in Chapter 4, algorithmic design works with large groups of designs called populations (Figure 4.16). Successive populations are generated, tested and winnowed with potentially no involvement on the part of the designer. The designer has absolutely no investment in any of the designs; thousands may be generated and rejected in the process of reaching a final, stable solution. Stability replaces the notion of the ideal.

The value that attaches to the final design is very different in each of these three cases. In the first, the design is an approximation of an ideal which exists, albeit vaguely, in the architect's mind. It is this ideal that drives design decisions and it is present in some way in the final design. In set-based design, performative factors have weighed very heavily in design decisions, if they have not driven them entirely. Rather than being the echo of an ideal, the final design is simply better than the alternatives. A stable solution emerges naturally from a long process of generation and selection. It is not the best alternative; it is the asymptotic termination of a series. It is certainly not the image of an ideal, since its designer could not have envisioned it.

Prospects

Some architects choose to continue to rely on drawing and work in the traditional manner. This needn't mean banning computers from the office, but using them as tools for drawing and physical model-making, rather than to model performance or generate form. Architects who take this path will find larger projects closed to them, and will have a limited clientele composed of people who understand architecture as representational. There will always be a certain number of such people, and a group of like-minded architects and critics to support this kind of work. The building industry as a whole, however, is in the process of abandoning traditional methods as owners increasingly make performance in its various guises the chief aim of their building projects. We are in the midst of the transition at this writing, but the conditions under which architecture will be practiced in the coming years are becoming clear. How architects will respond is the question. This is an extremely rare opportunity (the last one occurred over 500 years ago) for architecture to reinvent itself. Architects should be alive to the extraordinary opportunities at hand.

While operationalism and performativity shift the grounds on which architects may base their ideas, computational tools give them the ability to expand their field of operations and affect the conditions of building production as never before. Architects can question assumptions about the feasibility of building forms, the fabrication of systems and components, and methods of construction *and* implement new ideas on a project-by-project basis. This is *terra incognita*: traditional ideas do not necessarily apply here; architecture must find its way. It is very exciting, but poses the enormous challenge of using these new-found abilities in an intellectually responsible manner. Although BIM and computational design are the handmaidens of simulation, they can be directed towards other ends than the uncritical fulfillment of its demands. Taking their consequences seriously and using them knowingly can allow architects to take advantage of their power and at the same time reassert architecture as a potent cultural practice, a means of understanding the world we now find ourselves inhabiting, elucidating and affecting the choices we face.

Responsible exploration of these new abilities requires steering a course between the Scylla of wanton form-making and the Charybdis of capitulation to the demands of performativity. It also involves rethinking the relationship between architecture and the public. Architecture, like all art, has a responsibility to challenge its public. This entails a further responsibility to create buildings that make it rewarding to accept the challenge. There are at least three general approaches to this.

Preserving Representation

Architecture can open cracks in the nearly seamless simulation that envelopes our culture. Architects, by virtue of the persistence of representation in their discipline, are more likely than the general public to see simulation for what it is. To cultivate this awareness, architects need to find ways of neutralizing the performative tendencies of their tools. The key to preserving representation with BIM and computational design is to use them in conjunction with other media. If computer models are seen alongside drawings, analytical diagrams, physical models, material samples, photographs of precedents and context, and so on, they assume the aspect of being one way among many to understand a project, i.e. they become representations. Architecture schools should purposefully cultivate this attitude among their students, recognizing that they have many incoming students who experience the world as simulation. Once again putting drawing at the center of the curriculum is a vital part of this program. Likewise, architecture firms have to establish cultures in which multiple representations of every project are the norm. Architects need to take care that computer models are not accorded special status among the spectrum of representations and that the latter are used throughout the design and construction process, not only in its early stages. As a general practice, computer models should be displayed as abstractly as possible; renderings should be avoided until the design is well resolved by other means. Using a variety of media in presenting the project to clients and collaborators will help them see the models as representations as well. This is likely to encounter resistance on the part of some clients who expect to see finished images of their projects at their inception, but this is part of the attitude that is being challenged.

Asserting the role of the body in the experience of design and building exposes simulation and returns the design process to one of representation. A traditional design process based on drawings and physical models, valuing craftsmanship in their production, still seems the best way to do this. The computer would become essentially a support and documentation tool, and facilitate the production of models and full-scale mockups.

For any strategy of retaining representation, the problem of the subject arises: how can representation be asserted in a world dominated by simulation? The answer lies in the fact that the world is not yet entirely dominated by simulation. Writers like Baudrillard present simulation as a *fait accompli*, an epistemological cataclysm which has already destroyed the real and rendered our entire society incapable of comprehending the very notion of representation. This cannot be entirely true, else Baudrillard would not be able to place himself in a position to describe simulation. It is possible to position oneself outside of the regime of simulation by becoming aware of its operations. There are several centers of resistance to simulation in our society. Social and political movements that are critical of extant power structures and ideologies are naturally driven to call attention to and oppose simulation. Such critiques necessarily seek to expose deeper causes of events and dismantle performative logic. A prime example is environmentalism, which is engaged in a constant struggle to assert nature as a reality that exists outside of the view of it as raw material for human use.[10] In criticizing development projects on the grounds that they destroy a part of nature in pursuit of short-term gain, environmentalists are fundamentally objecting to the replacement of nature as a representation of values (beauty, wisdom, balance, harmony, etc.) by an operational view of nature that equates it with its use value. Similarly, anti-globalization or local empowerment movements criticize economic policies that take an operational view of wealth (as a means of achieving greater wealth) rather than understanding it as a resource for humanity at large to ensure its survival and happiness.

Another center of resistance is the culture of representation itself, preserved in academia, criticism, artistic practices of all kinds and a sizable portion of the public. The products of this culture are far less widely appreciated than more popular forms, and are often viewed as elitist. Nevertheless, it remains very strong, having the weight of the Western tradition behind it and a committed group of devotees who wield influence out of proportion to their number. In this scenario, architecture belongs to this culture, its mission to expose the workings of simulation, to provoke the public to step out of its customary mode of experience and take a fresh look at the world. Highlighting materials, traditional craftsmanship and the body; valuing such qualities as irregularity, approximation, and unpredictability are strategies to accomplish this.

Addressing Experience

In simulation we accept experience for itself, with no ulterior reality behind it. Architecture has always operated in this territory. Prior to any symbolism or signification, architecture affects us by shaping our spatial experience. Experience is the raw material that its representational functions draw upon. Experience is far from shallow; it is not simply physical stimuli, nor even those stimuli processed by the brain to create perception. There is a subject who sees, hears, touches, tastes, and smells, who experiences *qualities* in perception. The taste of chocolate, for example, is a distinctive, rich, yet indescribable experience. Most of us agree it tastes good, and we can describe it to some extent with such commonly understood qualities as sweetness and bitterness. But we have no way of knowing what someone else actually experiences when they take a bite. Gastronomy has a great deal to teach architecture in this regard. No one thinks a taste represents anything, yet the experience can be nuanced, unique, and laced with memory. Architecture has always played on this register of experience (Figure 6.14). Logocentrism has suppressed its celebration for centuries. Simulation may restore it to us.

Eliciting emotional response has always been a goal of architecture; for many architects, it is the highest goal. It was prominent in the thinking of Enlightenment architects such as Etienne-Louis Boullée[11] (Figure 2.30). It was also the essence of Le Corbusier's distinction between

FIGURe 6.14   Le Corbusier, Chapel of Nôtre Dame du Haut (c. 1954), interior. Geometry and history are present, but the patterns of colored glass and the deep wall recesses filled with light directly affect our senses and emotions.

Source: Photo by Rory Hyde.

architecture and the "Engineer's Esthetic."[12] Such thinking, however, is based on the notion that emotional responses to form are universal, so that architects who master composition can anticipate the response of the public to some extent. Our time recognizes social and cultural influences on perception and we therefore tend to reject such universal notions. This does not prevent contemporary architects from aiming for emotional responses to their work, but it does make guiding principles hard to come by.

Esthetics in our time has become both extremely unstable and highly personal. Mass media reduce esthetic ideas to the status of consumable images that are diffused widely and rapidly, going viral and then disappearing seemingly overnight. At the same time, an enormous variety of products is available, allowing people to feel that they are expressing their unique personalities by selective consumption. The rapid pace of change as well as the almost limitless variety of esthetic sensibilities poses great challenges for architects who would base their design practice on direct emotional appeal. Traditional buildings are too permanent to function as images in this environment but, reconceived as animated displays, they can respond to its demands (Figure 6.15, 6.16). Adaptive and responsive environments as well as ephemeral structures can also provide quickly changing environments (Figures 6.5, 6.6, 6.17). Lacking such animation, buildings tend to recede into the background, contributing to a general ambience but mute in themselves (Figure 6.8).

Another question for approaching architecture as the evocation of specific emotional responses has to do with the grounds for choosing a particular response. For a cenotaph (a recurring subject of Boullée's), the presence of death makes the choice of a somber, transcendental mood obvious. But for most projects, the choice is not as clear. Should an elementary school evoke the dignity of education, the amusement kids crave, respect for the institution, freedom of inquiry, or something else? The answer is probably "all of the above." It remains to be seen if this program can be successfully carried out, but the fundamental idea is consistent with the prevailing conditions.

FIGUrE 6.15   Times Square, New York City (2007). This classic urban space has been transformed into an animated electronic enclosure in which advertisements, signage and news flood the visitors' senses. The NASDAQ MarketSite (the cylindrical building at left) claims to be the world's largest stationary video screen at seven stories and an area of over 10,000 square feet. It comprises nearly 19 million LEDs.

Source: Photo by William Warby.

FIGURE 6.16 RTKL Architects, LA Live (c. 2010). "L.A. LIVE has established a premier 24/7 'Live, Work, Play Community' for the city of Los Angeles, transforming a previously underdeveloped industrial area into a vibrant urban district and economic engine" (from press release).

Source: © RTKL.com/David Whitcomb.

FIGURE 6.17 Kazuyo Sejima and Ryue Nishizawa, temporary pavilion, Serpentine Gallery, London (2009).

Source: Photo by Detlef Schobert.

Technology is opening up new types of spatial experience. Interactive, responsive and adaptive environments (Figures 6.5, 6.6) create dynamic relationships between people and their built environment that have only begun to be considered. So far these environments have been limited to the scope of installations. They have yet to be explored as a complete architecture.

Addressing the Problematics of Simulation

There are several problematics inherent in simulation that architecture can productively explore. One is the emerging hybrid nature of the subject, both of experience and design. On the experiential side, the electronic prostheses we are increasingly prone to wear will offer new avenues by which architects can affect their users' spatial experience (Figure 6.7). Architectural "interventions" in real environments will be possible by designing the information provided by such devices as Google Glass®. Already, GPS and apps like Google Maps and Yelp! subtly affect our perception of urban environments by transforming arbitrary locations into landmarks that rival Kevin Lynch's classic urban spatial structures that create our mental maps of a city.[13] While augmented reality has been explored as a medium for visualizing designs,[14] approaching such interventions as design opportunities in themselves is virgin territory for exploration by architects.

On the design side, the complex, flexible, pseudo-intelligent tool of the computer has begun to transform architects' thinking. The hypothesis that this collaboration produces a new, hybrid designing subject implies that a human with a computer is more than the simple sum of the two.[15] Computational design processes that combine the radically different capabilities of computer and human produce new species of forms whose cognitive bases are unfamiliar. We stand to learn a great deal about human cognition through the architectural investigation of this condition.

Other problematics can be found in algorithmic design and emergent form. These offer a new basis for architectural form, generating it from the conditions in which it exists rather than imposing pre-existing conceptions on it. This is nature's design strategy which always produces organisms precisely adapted to live in their environment. This strategy grounds architectural meaning, not in form as has traditionally been the case, but in relationships and processes. It requires architects to learn to think in terms of these rather than objects. It also requires a thorough understanding of computation. Whether and how people will learn to interpret the products of this approach to design is unknown at present. In adopting this approach, architects should bear in mind that the analogy between biological evolution and algorithmic design is a loose one. Evolutionary adaptation is determined by a very simple (and performative) criterion: the ability to survive and reproduce. Architectural adaptation is richer in its requirements. The selection criteria for any architectural form must be far more complex, involving social and cultural factors that do not lend themselves to being treated as species of performance.

Yet another problematic lies in the relationship between computational geometry and human perception. This "fourth geometry" as it has been called here, originates, not in our experience, but in the nature of computation applied to geometric operations. The fact that we find order in its products is remarkable if one accepts traditional explanations of the origins of geometric form as generalizations of human experience. The human mind can evidently recognize forms that bear little relationship to previous experience. In that it involves our perception of spatial order, this is a question that concerns architecture directly.

Other ways of thinking architecture in the age of simulation are no doubt possible. The only possibility that the discipline should not consider is allowing itself to be borne along by the current of performativity that is overtaking the building industry. That is the straight road to the extinction of the discipline. There is more to life than performance; there is more to meaning than operation.

Notes

1 The day when these too are embedded is not far off.
2 Carpo (2011).
3 Hollan, Hutchins, & Kirsch (2002).
4 Arias, Eden, Fischer, Gorman, & Scharff (2002).
5 Myers, Hudson, & Pausch (2002).
6 Cf. Harries (1997).
7 Cf. Heidegger (1977, 1993), Merleau-Ponty (1962), and Harries (1997).
8 Evans (1995, p. xxxi).
9 Husserl (1970, p. 26).
10 Heidegger (1977; 1993).

11 "Boullée set forth the laws of the beautiful as derived from nature in his 'theory of bodies', a study of the properties of objects laying emphasis on 'their power to stir our senses'" (Perouse de Montclos, 1974, p. 38).

12 Le Corbusier states:

> The Engineer, inspired by the law of economy and governed by mathematical calculation, puts us in accord with universal law. He achieves harmony.
>
> The Architect, by his arrangement of forms, realizes an order which is the pure creation of the spirit; by forms and shapes he affects our senses to an acute degree, and provokes plastic emotions; by the relationships which he creates he wakes in us profound echoes, he gives us the measure of an order which we feel to be in accordance with that of our world, he determines the various movements of our heart and of our understanding; it is then that we experience the sense of beauty.
>
> (Le Corbusier, 1986, p. 11)

13 Lynch (1960).

14 Fonseca, Marti, Navarro, Redondo, & Sanchez (2012).

15 The computer in this case is not simply automating and accelerating human cognitive tasks, but is allowing new cognitive processes to take place. This is not to say that computers are capable of cognition. Humans can conceive of cognitive processes that they themselves are not capable of carrying out, but that can be carried out for them by a computer. Cognition is always on the part of the human, first in conceiving the process and then in interpreting its results. The mechanics of the process are carried out by a computer.

POSTSCRIPT

The effects of simulation most immediately felt by architects are their clients' increasing demands for enhanced performance, both in their work processes and their buildings. Performance metrics are being applied to a growing number of aspects of building, as technologies evolve to provide the means of predicting and achieving building performance. Clients' expectations for accuracy in construction documents, cost estimates, and project schedules are rising, while their tolerance for unexpected changes is falling. The attempt to achieve the perennial goal of the perfect design has received fresh impetus from new tools that seem to offer the possibility its realization. This creates a cycle of improved tools, enhanced methods, better results, and higher expectations that focuses the industry's energy on meeting the performative demands of its clients. Many architects in the US seem to have been caught off guard by the suddenly elevated importance of performance in their work. It is not that they haven't been subjected to performance expectations before. They are used to meeting the demands of programs, schedules, and budgets. They are equally used to clients whose values skew towards the pragmatic or financial and who demonstrate little interest in other aspects of building. This experience, as frustrating as it can be, has not prevented the majority of architects from viewing their discipline as a fundamentally social and cultural enterprise, one which attempts to solve the ancient

Vitruvian problem of tempering necessity with a measure of delight, if not meaning. This attitude is described as humanist because it takes as its object the experience of human beings, experience that is emotional as well as concrete, social as well as personal, historically conditioned as well as universal.

Although they may not think of it in these terms, the changes entailed by simulation shock architects because of their anti-humanist implications. Simulation makes of performance an end in itself. Meaning is reduced to operation. The personal, the expressive, the idiosyncratic are denied legitimacy. Experience becomes hermetic, producing a frightening isolation. Even though these shifts are not yet complete, architects can feel them in the ways their position is being challenged. BIM presses the architect to become one among equals on teams that are unified by the desire to meet performance goals. The grounds on which expressive ends can be discussed are constantly eroded by the priority of performance benchmarks and ultimately confined to areas which performance has deemed unimportant. Computational design, when it is not being employed in service of explicitly performative ends, sublimates the architect's intentions so that they cannot be discerned in their products by a humanist subject.[1]

Simulation is a phenomenon, the result of concrete social and cultural developments. Most directly, simulation is a result of mass media that taught people to accept appearance as reality, to be satisfied with experience without context, to expand a small window so that it becomes a whole world. Now, of course, media are ubiquitous and so is the mode of experience we learned by consuming them. Simulation has become an integral part of our society and culture and cannot be separated from the whole messy, terrible, wonderful thing. The true origins of architects' discomfort with simulation, then, lie in the fundamental forces that shape our human world.

As building problems become increasingly complex technically, so does the daily work of architects, but our true responsibility remains the same: to think about *all* the consequences of design and construction decisions. We have belatedly come to the realization that how we build affects not only our own lives, but the life of every living thing on the planet. Architects understand that is not as much a technical issue as a moral one. As a society, we have made the uncritical assumption that performative goals are morally neutral, that they can always be made compatible with whatever values we wish to uphold. It should be clear by now that this is naïve. Values need to be defended and given force by adopting a critical stance towards performativity and simulation. If architects do not do this, no one in the building industry will.

Architects worry publicly these days about losing their position of leadership in the building industry, ceding the initiative on projects to contractors, construction managers, and owners' representatives. The most common response is that we architects must provide owners with greater assurances of performance in our work and products. While architects should use—and improve—the tools available, we will not solve our problem by outdoing contractors by becoming more-performative-than-thou. The real challenge is that simulation is cutting the ground from under the very modes of thought that we architects have applied to building. We need to re-establish or find new grounds for our work. We need to double down on design: re-think what building means now, how the built environment affects not only people but the entire ecosystem. We need to challenge people, as we always have with our best work, and adopt positions alongside simulation that allow us to understand and critique its effects. Drawing will be a powerful tool in doing this.

This is a most challenging time to be an architect. We architects must take up the challenge, work to understand the emerging world, find new ideas and create pragmatic positions from which we can effectively shape a world worth living in. The world needs architects and architecture as never before.

Note

1 These new conditions partially describe what is known to some social and architectural critics as post-humanism. cf. Eisenman (1998). Yet even such critics insist on the architect's prerogative as the form-giver.

BIBLIOGRAPHY AND FURTHER READING

Abouelkheir, A., Shahi, B., Lee, J.-A., & Wong, P. (2012). "Terriform." *ACADIA 2012 Synthetic Digital Landscapes*. San Francisco: 35Degree.

Alberti, L. B. (1966). *On Painting*. New Haven, CT: Yale University Press.

Alberti, L. B. (1988). *On the Art of Building in Ten Books*. (J. Rykwert, N. Leach, & R. Tavernor, trans.) Cambridge, MA: The MIT Press.

Alexander, C. (1964). *Notes on the Synthesis of Form*. Cambridge, MA: Harvard University Press.

Alexander, C. (2011). "Systems Generating Systems." In A. Menges, & S. Ahlquist, *Computational Design Thinking* (pp. 58–67). Chichester: John Wiley & Sons.

American Institute of Architects, AIA California Council. (2007). *Integrated Project Delivery: A Guide*. Washington, DC: American Institute of Architects.

Arias, E., Eden, H., Fischer, G., Gorman, A., & Scharff, E. (2002). "Transcending the Individual Human Mind: Creating Shared Understanding through Collaborative Design." In J. M. Carroll (Ed.), *Human-Computer Interaction in the New Millenium*. New York: Addison-Wesley.

Arthur, B. (2009). *The Nature of Technology: What It Does and How It Evolves*. New York: Free Press.

Banham, R. (1969). *The Architecture of the Well-Tempered Environment*. London: The Architectural Press/Chicago: University of Chicago Press.

Barthes, R., Lavers, A., & Smith, C. (1999). *Elements of Semiology* (21st printing ed.). New York: Hill and Wang.

Baudrillard, J. (1994). *Simulacra and Simulation*. Ann Arbor: The University of Michigan Press.

Bhooshan, S. (2013, June 25). "Learning from Candela." (D. R. Scheer, Interviewer).

Bovelet, J. (2010). "Drawing as Epistemic Practice in Architectural Design." *Footprint, 4*(7), 75–84.

Building Design and Construction. (2010, August 11). *BD+C Weekly Newsletter*. Available at: http://www.bdcnetwork.com/bim-adoption-tops-80-among-nations-largest-aec-firms-according-bdcs-giants-300-survey (accessed November 7, 2012).

Carpo, M. (2011). *The Alphabet and the Algorithm*. Cambridge, MA: The MIT Press.

Construction Users Roundtable. (2004). *Collaboration, Integrated Information and the Project Lifecycle in Building Design, Construction and Operation*. Cincinnati: The Construction Users Roundtable.

Cuff, D. (1991). *Architecture: The Story of Practice*. Cambridge, MA: The MIT Press.

Danto, A. C. (1986). *The Philosophical Disenfranchisement of Art*. New York: Columbia University Press.

deLanda, M. (2002). "Deleuze and the Use of the Genetic Algorithm in Architecture." In N. Leach, *Designing for a Digital World*. London: John Wiley & Sons.

deLanda, M. (2011). *Philosophy and Simulation: The Emergence of Synthetic Reason*. New York: Continuum International Publishing Group.

Derrida, J. (1981). *Positions*. Chicago: University of Chicago Press.

Deutsch, R. (2011). *BIM and Integrated Design:Strategies for Architectural Practice*. Hoboken, NJ: Wiley.

Eastman, C., Teicholz, P., Sacks, R., & Liston, K. (2011). *BIM Handbook* (2nd ed.). Hoboken: John Wiley & Sons, Inc.

Eisenman, P. (1976). "Post-Functionalism." *Oppositions* (6).

Eisenman, P. (1998). "The End of the Classical: The End of the Beginning, the End of the End." In K. M. Hays, *Architecture Theory Since 1968*. Cambridge, MA: MIT Press.

Eklund, P., & Haemmerle, O. e. (2008). "Conceptual Structures: Knowledge Visualization and Reasoning." In *International Conference on Conceptual Structures*. Berlin; Springer.

Ellul, J. (1964). *The Technological Society*. New York: Alfred A. Knopf, Inc.

Environmental Design Research Association. (n.d.). *EDRA*. Available at: www.edra.org (accessed May 16, 2013).

Euclid. (1956). *The Thirteen Books of the Elements* (2 ed., Vol. 1). (S. T. Heath, Ed.) New York: Dover Publications, Inc.

Evans, R. (1995). *The Projective Cast: Architecture and Its Three Geometries*. Cambridge, MA: The MIT Press.

Evans, R. (1997). "Translations from Drawings to Buildings." In R. Evans, *Translations from Drawings to Buildings and Other Essays*. London: Architectural Association Publications.

Finau, E., & Lee, Y. C. (n.d.). "BIM Enabled Lean Construction: Faster, Easier, Better and Less Expensive Project Delivery." Online, Georgia Tech. Available at: dbl.gatech.edu: http://www.dbl.gatech.edu/sites/www.dbl.gatech.edu/files/Lee-Finau.pdf (accessed July 25, 2013).

Fischer, O. W. (2012). "Architecture, Capitalism and Criticality." In C. G. Crysler, S. Cairns, & H. Heynen (Eds.), *The SAGE Handbook of Architectural Theory*. London: SAGE Publications, Ltd.

Fitzsimons, J. K. (2010). "The Body Drawn between Knowledge and Desire." *Footprint, 4*(7), 9–28.

Fonseca, D., Marti, N., Navarro, I., Redondo, E., & Sanchez, A. (2012). "Using Augmented Reality and Education Platform in Architectural Visualization: Evaluation of Usability and Student's Level of Satisfaction." In *2012 International Symposium on Computers in Education (SIIE)*. Andorra la Vella: IEEE.

Foucault, M. (1973). *The Order of Things*. New York: Random House, Inc.

Foucault, M. (1979). *Discipline and Punish*. New York: Knopf Doubleday Publishing Group.

Frascari, M. (2007). "Introduction: Models and Drawings: The Invisible Nature of Architecture." In J. H. Marco Frascari (Ed.), *From Models to Drawing*. London: Routledge.

Frazer, J. (2011). "A Natural Model for Architecture." In A. Menges, & S. Ahlquist, *Computational Design Thinking*. Chichester: John Wiley & Sons.

Gallaher, M. P., Dettbarn, J. L., & Gilday, L. T. (2004). *Cost Analysis of Inadequate Interoperability in the U.S. Capital Facilities Industry*. Gaithersburg: National Institute of Standards and Technology.

Giedion, S. (1978). *Space, Time and Architecture*. Cambridge, MA: Harvard University Press.

Gleick, J. (1987). *Chaos: Making a New Science*. New York: The Penguin Group.

Haptic & Embedded Mechatronics Laboratory. (n.d.). *Haptic Shear Feedback*. Available at: http://heml.eng.utah.edu/index.php/Haptics/ShearFeedback (accessed June 27, 2013).

Harries, K. (1997). *The Ethical Function of Architecture*. Cambridge, MA: The MIT Press.

Heidegger, M. (1962). *Being and Time*. (J. Macquarrie, & E. Robinson, Trans.) San Francisco: Harper & Row.

Heidegger, M. ([1977a,] 1993). "Building, Dwelling, Thinking." In D. F. Krell (Ed.), *Martin Heidegger: Basic Writings*. San Francisco: HarperSanFrancisco.

Heidegger, M. ([1977b] 1993). "The Question Concerning Technology." In D. F. Krell (Ed.), *Martin Heidegger: Basic Writings*. San Francisco: HarperSanFrancisco.

Heumann, A. (2012). "Michael Graves: Digital Visionary: What Digital Design Practice Can Learn from Drawing." Available at: http://acadia.org/#features/ H76XXP (accessed February 12, 2013).

Hollan, J., Hutchins, E., & Kirsch, D. (2002). "Distributed Cognition: Toward a New Foundation for Human-Computer Interaction Research." In J. M. Carroll (Ed.), *Human-Computer Interaction in the New Millenium*. New York: Addison-Wesley.

Hsiao, C.-P., Davis, N., & Do, E. Y.-L. (2012). "Dancing on the Desktop: Gesture Modeling System to Augment Design Cognition." In *Synthetic Digital*

Ecologies: Proceedings of the 32nd Annual Conference of the Association for Computer-Aided Design in Architecture (ACADIA). San Francisco: Association for Computer-Aided Design in Architecture (ACADIA).

Husserl, E. (1970). *The Crisis of European Sciences and Transcendental Phenomenology*. (D. Carr, Trans.) Evanston, IL: Northwestern University Press.

Ibbitson, T. (2013, July 28). *BIM: Defining Value*. Available at: FreeArchitecture. org.UK/: http://freearchitecture.org.uk/bim-defining-value/ (accessed August 8, 2013).

Iwamoto, T., Tatezono, M., Hoshi, T., & Shinoda, H. (2008). "Touchable Holography." Available at: http://www.alab.t.u-tokyo.ac.jp/~siggraph/09/TouchableHolography/SIGGRAPH09-TH.html (accessed June 27, 2013).

Kahn, L. I. (1991). *Writings, Lectures, Interviews*. New York: Rizzoli International Publications, Inc.

Kant, I. (1929). *Critique of Pure Reason*. (N. K. Smith, Trans.). New York: The Humanities Press.

Kaufmann, E. (1952). "Three Revolutionary Architects: Boullee, Ledoux and Lequeu." *Transactions of the American Philosophical Society, New Series, 42*(3), 431–564.

Kieran, S., & Timberlake, J. (2004). *Refabricating Architecture*. New York: McGraw-Hill.

Kimmelman, M. (2012, October 31). "Barclays Center Arena and Atlantic Yards Project in Brooklyn." NYTimes.com. Available at: http://www.nytimes.com/2012/11/01/arts/design/barclays-center-arena-and-atlantic-yards-project-in-brooklyn.html?pagewanted=all&_r=0 (accessed May 21, 2013).

Kolarevic, B. (2005). "Towards the Performative in Architecture." In B. Kolarevic & A. M. Malkawi, *Performative Architecture: Beyond Instrumentality*. New York: Spon Press.

Kuorikoski, J. (2012). "Simulation and the Sense of Understanding." In P. A. Humphreys, *Models, Simulations, and Representations*. New York: Routledge.

Leatherbarrow, D. (2005). "Architecture's Unscripted Performance." In B. Kolarevic, & A. M. Malkawi, *Performative Architecture: Beyond Instrumentality*. New York: Spon Press.

Le Corbusier, P. J. (1986). *Towards a New Architecture*. New York: Dover Publications, Inc.

Levin, D. M. (1993). "Introduction." In D. M. Levin (Ed.), *Modernity and the Hegemony of Vision*. Berkeley: The University of California Press.

Loughborough University; Foster + Partners; Buro Happold. (2010, May 29). "Future of Construction Process: 3D Concrete Printing." Available at: http://www.youtube.com/watch?v=EfbhdZKPHro (accessed July 30, 2013).

Lynch, K. (1960). *The Image of the City*. Cambridge, MA: Technology Press.

Lyotard, J.-F. (1984). *The Postmodern Condition: A Report on Knowledge*. Minneapolis: The University of Minnesota Press.

Marin, P. (2001). *On Representation*. Stanford, CA: Stanford University Press.

McCullough, M. (1998). *Abstracting Craft.* Cambridge, MA: The MIT Press.

McGraw-Hill Construction. (2009). *The Business Value of BIM.* New York: McGraw-Hill.

Mendelsohn, D. (2012). *Waiting for the Barbarians: Essays from the Classics to Pop Culture.* New York: New York Review of Books.

Menges, A. (2011). "Integral Formation and Materialization." In A. Menges, & S. Ahlquist, *Computational Design Thinking.* Chichester: John Wiley & Sons.

Menges, A., & Ahlquist, S. (2011a). *Computational Design Thinking.* Chichester: John Wiley & Sons.

Menges, A., & Ahlquist, S. (2011b). "Introduction: Computational Design Thinking." In A. Menges, & S. Ahlquist, *Computational Design Thinking.* Chichester: John Wiley & Sons.

Merleau-Ponty, M. (1962). *The Phenomenology of Perception.* London: Routledge & Kegan Paul Ltd.

Miller, N. (2012a). Interview with D. Scheer, October 19, 2012.

Miller, N. (2012b). "Algorithms Are Thoughts: Design Thinking in an Automated World." Available at: YouTube: https://www.youtube. com/watch?v=OE1imo HkS-8 (accessed December 10, 2013).

Myers, B., Hudson, S. E., & Pausch, R. (2002). Past, Present and Future of Interface Software Tools. In J. M. Carroll (Ed.), *Human-Computer Interaction in the New Millenium.* New York: Addison-Wesley.

Naylor, B. (2008, February 22). "Introduction to Computational Representations of Geometry." Available at: 13th monkey.org: http://www.13thmonkey.org/ documentation/CAD/ (accessed December 17, 2012).

Negro, F. (2012). "Unprecedented Value." Available at: https://higherlogic download.s3.amazonaws.com/AIA/5%20-%20Unprecedented%20Value% 20-%20NEGRO1.pdf?AWSAccessKeyId=AKIAJH5D4I4FWRALBOUA& Expires=1375994405&Signature=XzmdN%2BfH0iWDlmQuOeqzRsMiuwQ% 3D (accessed May 12, 2013).

Negroponte, N. (1969, September). "Towards a Humanism through Machines." *Architectural Design,* 511–512.

Nicolis, G., & Prigogine, I. (1989). *Exploring Complexity: An Introduction.* New York: W. H. Freeman & Company.

Pallasmaa, J. (2009). *The Thinking Hand.* Chichester: John Wiley & Sons, Ltd.

Pauly, D. (1997). *Le Corbusier: The Chapel at Ronchamp.* Basel: Verlag für Architektur.

Perez-Gomez, A. (1983). *Architecture and the Crisis of Modern Science.* Cambridge, MA: The MIT Press.

Perez-Gomez, A., & Pelletier, L. (1997). *Architectural Representation and the Perspective Hinge.* Cambridge, MA: The MIT Press.

Perouse de Montclos, J.-M. (1974). *Etienne-Louis Boullee: Theoretician of Revolutionary Architecture.* New York: George Braziller.

Pinker, S. (1994). *The Language Instinct.* New York: HarperCollins.

Plato (1965). *Timaeus and Critias.* London: Penguin Books.

Provancher, W. (2013, June 17). "Reactive Grip Tactile Feedback for Precision Manipulation." Available at: http://www.youtube.com/watch?v=oKIPr5eEJtQ &feature=youtube (accessed June 29, 2013).

Ramsey, D. (2008, September 17). "3D Virtual Reality Environment Developed at UC San Diego Helps Scientists Innovate." Available at: *UC San Diego News*: http://ucsdnews.ucsd.edu/newsrel/general/09-083DVirtualReality.asp (accessed December 31, 2012).

Rosenau, H. (Ed.). (1953). *Boullée's Treatise on Architecture, a Complete Presentation of the "Architecture: Essai sur l'art," which Forms a Part of the Boullée Papers (MS 9153) in the Bibliothèque Nationale, Paris*. London: Alex Tiranti.

Saussure, F. de (1966). *Course in General Linguistics*. New York: Philosophical Library.

Scheer, D. (1992, Spring). "Critical Differences: Notes on a Comparative Study of French and U.S. Practice." *Practices, 1*(1), 31–40.

Sennett, R. (2008). *The Craftsman*. New Haven, CT: Yale University Press.

Shinoda Lab, University of Tokyo. (2009, July 16). "Touchable Holography." Available at: http://www.youtube.com/watch?v=Y-P1zZAcPuw (accessed June 29, 2013).

Singer, D. J., Doerry, N., & Buckley, M. E. (2009). "What is Set-Based design?" *Naval Engineers Journal, 121*(4), 31–43.

Terzides, K. (2006). *Algorithmic Architecture*. Amsterdam: Elsevier Architectural Press.

Terzides, K. (2011). "Algorithmic Form." In A. Menges, & S. Ahlquist, *Computational Design Thinking* (pp. 94–101). Chichester: John Wiley & Sons.

Tombesi, P. (2001). "A True South for Design? The New International Division of Labour in Architecture." *Architectural Research Quarterly, 5*(2), 171–180.

Tufte, E. R. (1983). *The Visual Display of Quantitative Information*. Cheshire, CT: Graphics Press.

Turkle, S. (2009). *Simulation and Its Discontents*. Cambridge, MA: The MIT Press.

Venturi, R. (1966). *Complexity and Contradiction in Architecture*. New York: Museum of Modern Art

Venturi, R., Izenour, S., Scott-Brown, D. (1977) *Learning from Las Vegas: The Forgotten Symbolism of Architectural Form. Revised Edition*. Cambridge: MIT Press.

Vonnegut, K. (1963). *Cat's Cradle*. New York: Holt, Rinehart and Winston.

Wittgenstein, L. (1922). *Tractatus Logico-Philosophicus*. New York: Harcourt-Brace & Company, Inc.

Wittkower, R. (1971). *Architectural Principles in the Age of Humanism*. New York: Norton Library.

Woodbury, R. (2010). *Elements of Parametric Design*. New York: Routledge.

INDEX